RAJASTHAN

A STATE STUDY GUIDE

LALIT MOHAN SHEKHAWAT

Published by

Hawk Press
4836/24, Ansari Road, Daryaganj
New Delhi – 110 002
Phones: 91-11-23278618, 91-11-43667199
E-mail: thehawkpress@gmail.com
www.thehawkpress.com

ISBN: 978-93-88318-88-4

Preface

Rajasthan, state of northwestern India, located in the northwestern part of the Indian subcontinent. It is bounded to the north and northeast by the states of Punjab and Haryana, to the east and southeast by the states of Uttar Pradesh and Madhya Pradesh, to the southwest by the state of Gujarat, and to the west and northwest by the provinces of Sindh and Punjab in Pakistan. The capital city is Jaipur, in the east-central part of the state.

This book dwells on the history of Rajasthan which has a unique historical character and is deeply connected with the race of Rajputs who through their bravery and valour have faced the onslaughts of the Muslim Invaders through-out the Centuries. Besides this the people of Rajasthan are very advanced in Folk Culture and they are considered to be great Craftsman.

Rajasthan, meaning "The Abode of the Rajas," was formerly called Rajputana, "The Country of the Rajputs" (sons of rajas [princes]). Before 1947, when India achieved independence from British rule, it comprised some two dozen princely states and chiefships, the small British-administered province of Ajmer-Merwara, and a few pockets of territory outside the main boundaries. After 1947 the princely states and chiefships were integrated into India in stages, and the state took the name Rajasthan. It assumed its present form on November 1, 1956, when the States Reorganization Act came into force. Area 132,139 square miles (342,239 square km). Pop. (2011) 68,621,012.

The agricultural sector has long been the mainstay of Rajasthan's economy. It accounts for about one-fourth of the state's economic output, employing about two-thirds of the state's working population. Despite scant and scattered rainfall, nearly all types of crops are grown, including pearl millet in the desert area, sorghum around Kota, and mainly corn (maize) around Udaipur.

Rajasthan is one of the most popular tourist destinations in India, for both domestic and international tourists. Rajasthanattracts tourists for its historical forts, palaces, art and culture with its slogan 'Padharo mahare desh'. Every third foreign tourist visiting India travels to Rajasthan as it is part of the Golden Triangle for tourists visiting India.

The structure of Rajasthan's government, like that of most other states in India, is determined by the national constitution of 1950. The head of state is the governor, who is appointed by the president of India for a five-year term. The governor is aided and advised by the Council of Ministers, which is headed by a chief minister and is responsible to the unicameral Legislative Assembly (Vidhan Sabha); members are elected by universal adult franchise, although some seats are reserved for representatives of tribal groups (Scheduled Tribes) and other traditionally disadvantaged communities (Scheduled Castes).

A History of Rajasthan uses various archival, epigraphical, numismatical, architectural, archaeological, and art-history related information as well as traditional narratives, and oral and written chronicles, to provide a general overview of aspects like literature, religion, art and architecture, position of women, socio-economic conditions, science and technology, as well as the subaltern, peoples' oriented, 'everyday' life of the 'average citizen'.

This is a reference book. All the matter is just compiled and edited in nature, taken from the various sources which are in public domain.

The book deals with history, geography, economy, districts, power situation, small industries development, social welfare schemes and tourism.

—Editor

ABOUT THE BOOK

Rajasthan which is also known as the "Land of Maharajas" is the largest state of India, covering an area of about 342,239 sq. km. It comprises of 33 districts and its largest city is Jaipur, which is also its capital. Being located on the western side of the country, it shares its border with Pakistan to its northwest and to the west it shares its border with Sindh. Rajasthan is a land of history and romance. It has always played a pivotal role in boosting the arts and culture of India and is deservedly a tourists' paradise of India. The echo of the changing swords and the beat of war drums is ever present, but the thunks of the sculptor's chisel, the rustle of a painter's brush, the melody of a musicein's notes and the jingle of the dancer's anklets have also been heard here. Some of its major architectural wonders include Chittorgarh fort - the largest fort in Asia, Mehrangarh Fort at Jodhpur, Jaipur "The Pink City" houses a number of well known tourists spots which include Hawa Mahal (Palace of Winds), Lake Palace, City Palace, Amber Palace, Jantar Mantar, Umaid Bhawan in Jodhpur, Jaisalmer Fort in Jaisalmer and many more. A History of Rajasthan uses various archival, epigraphical, numismatical, architectural, archaeological, and art-history related information as well as traditional narratives, and oral and written chronicles, to provide a general overview of aspects like literature, religion, art and architecture, position of women, socio-economic conditions'.

Contents

1

State at a Glance

Rajasthan is a state in the north western region of India. The state covers an area of 342,239 square kilometres (132,139 sq mi) or 10.4 percent of the total geographical area of India. It is the largest Indian state by area and the seventh largest by population. Rajasthan is located on the northwestern side of India, where it comprises most of the wide and inhospitable Thar Desert (also known as the "Rajasthan Desert" and "Great Indian Desert") and shares a border with the Pakistani provinces of Punjab to the northwest and Sindh to the west, along the Sutlej-Indusriver valley. Elsewhere it is bordered by five other Indian states: Punjab to the north; Haryana and Uttar Pradesh to the northeast; Madhya Pradesh to the southeast; and Gujarat to the southwest.

Major features include the ruins of the Indus Valley Civilisation at Kalibanga; the Dilwara Temples, a Jain pilgrimage site at Rajasthan's only hill station, Mount Abu, in the ancient Aravalli mountain range; and, in eastern Rajasthan, the Keoladeo National Park near Bharatpur, a World Heritage Site known for its bird life. Rajasthan is also home to three national tiger reserves, the Ranthambore National Park in Sawai Madhopur, Sariska Tiger Reserve in Alwar and Mukundra Hill Tiger Reserve in Kota.

The state was formed on 30 March 1949 when Rajputana – the name adopted by the British Raj for its dependencies in the region – was merged into the Dominion of India. Its capital and largest city is Jaipur. Other important cities are Jodhpur, Kota, Bikaner, Ajmer and Udaipur.

ETYMOLOGY

Rajasthan literally means "Land of Kings" or "King's Abode" (from *raja* "king" and *-sthan land, abode" from Sanskrit* sthâìna*)*.

The first mention of the name "Rajasthan" appears in the 1829 publication *Annals and Antiquities of Rajast'han or the Central and Western Rajpoot States of India*, while the earliest known record of "Rajputana" as a name for the region is in George Thomas's 1800 memoir *Military Memories*. John Keay, in his book *India: A History*, stated that "Rajputana" was coined by the British in 1829, John Briggs, translating Ferishta's history of early Islamic India, used the phrase "Rajpoot (Rajput) princes" rather than "Indian princes".

HISTORY OF RAJASTHAN

Ancient

Parts of what is now Rajasthan were partly part of the Vedic Civilisation and Indus Valley Civilization. Kalibangan, in Hanumangarh district, was a major provincial capital of the Indus Valley Civilization.

Stone Age tools dating from 5,000 to 2,00,000 years were found in Bundi and Bhilwara districts of the state.

Matsya Kingdom of the Vedic civilisation of India, is said to roughly corresponded to the former state of Jaipur in Rajasthan and included the whole of Alwar with portions of Bharatpur. The capital of Matsya was at Viratanagar (modern Bairat), which is said to have been named after its founder king Virata.

Bhargava identifies the two districts of Jhunjhunu and Sikar and parts of Jaipur district along with Haryana districts of Mahendragarh and Rewari as part of Vedic state of Brahmavarta. Bhargava also locates the present day Sahibi River as the Vedic Drishadwati River, which along with Saraswati River formed the borders of the Vedic state of Brahmavarta. Manu and Bhrigunarrated the Manusmriti to a congregation of seers in this area only. Ashrams of Vedic seers Bhrigu and his son Chayvan Rishi, for whom Chyawanprash was formulated, were near Dhosi Hill part of which lies in Dhosi village of Jhunjhunu district of Rajasthan and part lies in Mahendragarh district of Haryana.

The Western Kshatrapas (405–35 BC), the Saka rulers of the western part of India, were successors to the Indo-Scythians, and were contemporaneous with the Kushans, who ruled the northern part of the Indian subcontinent. The Indo-Scythians invaded the area of Ujjain and established the Saka era (with their calendar), marking the beginning of the long-lived Saka Western Satraps state.

Classical

Gurjars

Gurjars ruled for many dynasties in this part of the country, the region was known as *Gurjaratra*. Up to the 10th century AD, almost all of North India acknowledged the supremacy of the Gurjars, with their seat of power at Kannauj.

Gurjara-Pratihara

The Gurjar Pratihar Empire acted as a barrier for Arab invaders from the 8th to the 11th century. The chief accomplishment of the Gurjara-Pratihara Empire lies in its successful resistance to foreign invasions from the west, starting in the days of Junaid. Historian R. C. Majumdar says that this was openly acknowledged by the Arab writers.

He further notes that historians of India have wondered at the slow progress of Muslim invaders in India, as compared with their rapid advance in other parts of the world. Now there seems little doubt that it was the power of the Gurjara Pratihara army that effectively barred the progress of the Arabs beyond the confines of Sindh, their only conquest for nearly 300 years.

Medieval and Early Modern

Historical tribes

Traditionally the Rajputs, Gurjars, Jats, Meenas, Bhils, Rajpurohit, Charans, Yadavs, Bishnois, Meghwal, Sermals, PhulMali (Saini) and other tribes made a great contribution in building the state of Rajasthan. All these tribes suffered great difficulties in protecting their culture and the land. Millions of them were killed trying to protect their land. Bhils once ruled Kota. Meenas were rulers of Bundi, Hadoti and the Dhundhar region.

Major rulers

- Hemu, the Hindu Emperor, was born in the village of Machheri in Alwar District in 1501. He won 22 battles against Afghans, from Punjab to Bengalincluding states of Ajmer and Alwar in Rajasthan, and defeated Akbar's forces twice at Agra and Delhi in 1556 at Battle of Delhi before acceding to the throne of Delhi and establishing the "Hindu Raj" in North India, albeit for a short duration, from Purana Quila in Delhi. Hem Chandra was killed in the battlefield at Second Battle of Panipat fighting against Mughals on 5 November 1556.
- Maharana Pratap of Mewar resisted Akbar in the famous Battle of Haldighati (1576) and later operated from hilly areas of his kingdom. The Bhils were Maharana's main allies during these wars. Most of these attacks were repulsed even though the Mughal forces outnumbered Mewar Rajputs in all the wars fought between them. The Haldighati war was fought between 10,000 Mewaris and a 100,000-strong Mughal force (including many Rajputs like Kachwahas from Dhundhar).
- Jat king Maharaja Suraj Mal (February 1707 – 25 December 1764) or *Sujan Singh* was ruler of Bharatpur in Rajasthan. A contemporary historian has described him as "the Plato of the Jat people" and by a modern

writer as the "Jat Odysseus", because of his political sagacity, steady intellect, and clear vision.

Rajput martial history

Rajput families rose to prominence in the 6th century CE. The Rajputs put up resistance to the Islamic invasions with their warfare and chivalry for centuries. During the 12th century, the Turks and Afghans were able to get a firm grip on Punjab, Delhi and Bengal. The Rana's of Mewar led other kingdoms in its resistance to outside rule. Rana Hammir Singh, defeated the Tughlaq dynasty and recovered a large portion of Rajasthan. The indomitable Rana Kumbha defeated the Sultans of Malwa and Gujarat and made Mewar the most powerful Rajput Kingdom in India. The ambitious Rana Sanga united the various Rajput clans and fought against the foreign powers in India. Rana Sanga defeated the Afghan Lodi Empire of Delhi and crushed the Turkic Sultanates of Malwa and Gujarat. Rana Sanga then tried to create an Indian empire but was defeated by the first Mughal Emperor Babur at Khanua. The defeat was due to betrayal by the Tomar king Silhadi of Raisen. After Rana Sangas death there was no one who could check the rapid expansion of the Mughal Empire.

During Akbars reign most of the Rajput kings accepted Mughal Suzerainty, but the rulers of Mewar (Rana Udai Singh II) and Marwar (Rao Chandrasen Rathore) refused to have any form of alliance with the Mughals. To teach the Rajputs a lesson Akbar attacked Udai Singh and killed Rajput commander Jaimal of Chitor and the citizens of Mewar in large numbers. Akbar killed 20 – 25,000 unarmed citizens in Chittor on the grounds that they had actively helped in the resistance.

Maharana Pratap took an oath to avenge the citizens of Chittor, he fought the Mughal empire till his death and liberated most of Mewar apart from Chittor itself. Maharana Pratap soon became the most celebrated warrior of Rajasthan and became famous all over India for his sporadic warfare and noble actions. According to Satish Chandra, "Rana Pratap's defiance of the mighty Mughal empire, almost alone and unaided by the other Rajput states, constitutes a glorious saga of Rajput valour and the spirit of self sacrifice for cherished principles. Rana Pratap's methods of sporadic warfare was later elaborated further by Malik Ambar, the Deccani general, and by Shivaji".

Rana Amar Singh I continued his ancestors war against the Mughal's under Jehangir, he repelled the Mughal armies at Dewar. Later an expedition was again sent under leadership of Prince Khurram, which caused much damage to life and property of Mewar. Many temples were destroyed, several villages were put on fire and ladies and children were captured and tortured to make Amar Singh accept surrender.

During Aurangzebs rule Rana Raj Singh I and Veer Durgadas Rathore were chief among those who defied the intolerant emperor of Delhi. They took advantage of the Aravalli hills and caused heavy damage on the Mughal armies that were trying to occupy Rajasthan.

Hawa Mahal ("Palace of Winds") in Jaipur

After Aurangzebs death Bahadur Shah I tried to subjugate Rajasthan like his ancestors but his plan backfired when the three Rajput Raja's of Amber, Udaipur and Jodhpur made a joint resistance to the Mughals. The Rajputs first expelled the commandants of Jodhpur and Bayana and recovered Amer by a night attack. They next killed Sayyid Hussain Khan Barha, the commandant of Mewat and many other Mughal officers. Bahadur Shah I, then in the Deccan was forced to patch up a truce with the Rajput Rajas.

Over the years, the Mughals began to have internal disputes which greatly distracted them at times. The Mughal Empire continued to weaken, and with the decline of the Mughal Empire in the late 18th century, Rajputana came under the influence of the Marathas. The Maratha Empire, which had replaced the Mughal Empire as the overlord of the subcontinent, was finally replaced by the British Empire in 1818.

The Mehrangarh Fort at Jodhpurwas built by Rao Jodha in 1459.

In the 19th century the Rajput kingdoms were exhausted, they had been drained financially and in manpower after continuous wars and due to heavy tributes exacted by the Maratha Empire. In order to save their kingdoms from instability, rebellions and banditry the Rajput kings concluded treaties with the British in the early 19th century, accepting British suzerainty and control over their external affairs in return for internal autonomy.

Modern

Modern Rajasthan includes most of Rajputana, which comprises the erstwhile nineteen princely states, two chiefships, and the British district of Ajmer-Merwara. Jaisalmer, Marwar (Jodhpur), Bikaner, Mewar (Chittorgarh), Alwar and Dhundhar (Jaipur) were some of the main Rajput princely states. Bharatpur and Dholpur were Jat princely states whereas Tonk was a princely state under a Muslim Nawab.

Rajasthan's formerly independent kingdoms created a rich architectural and cultural heritage, seen even today in their numerous forts and palaces (Mahals and Havelis), which are enriched by features of Rajput and Jain architecture.

The development of frescos in Rajasthan is linked with the history of the Marwaris (Jodhpur-pali), who played a crucial role in the economic development of the region.

RAJASTHAN RICH HISTORY AND HERITAGE

Ancient history

The ancient civilised history of Rajasthan goes back to 5,000 years ago when in the present day districts of Jhunjhunu and Sikar, along with other areas of Jaipur district bordering south Haryana, which formed the part of Vedic state of Brahmavartaalong with districts of Mahendragarh and Rewari in Haryana, that Vedic seers started composing Vedic scriptures, which form part of Sanatan Dharma, the base of present day Hinduism. Revered Saraswati and Drishadwati rivers formed the then Brahmavarta state. Drishadwati river is identified as the Vedic Drishadwati by Bhargava. Parts of Rajasthan may have been occupied by the Indus Valley Civilization (Harappans). Excavations at Kalibanga in northern Rajasthan around 1998 revealed the existence of human settlements of Harappan times on the banks of a river that dried up later, which some people believe to be the Saraswati, archaeologists hope the Saraswati will unlock mysteries of the past. Rajasthan's geographic position in India has caused it to be affected by the expansionist efforts of various empires. It was a part of the Maurya Empire around 321-184 BCE.

Medieval period

Prithviraj Chauhan defeated the invading Muhammad Ghori in the first battle of Tarain in 1191. In 1192 CE,Muhammad Ghori decisively defeated Prithviraj at the Second battle of Tarain.

After the defeat of Chauhan in 1192 CE, a part of Rajasthan came under Muslim rulers. The principal centers of their powers were Nagaur and Ajmer. Ranthambhor was also under their suzerainty. At the beginning of the 13th century, the most prominent and powerful state of Rajasthan was Mewar. The Rajputs resisted the Muslim incursions into India, although a number of Rajput kingdoms eventually became subservient to the Delhi Sultanate. Mewar led others in resistance to Muslim rule: Rana Sanga united the various Rajput clans and fought against the foreign powers in India. Rana Sanga defeated the Afghan Lodi Empire of Delhi and crushed the Turkic Sultanates of Malwa and Gujarat. Rana Sanga was later defeated at Khanwa against the Mughal Empire because of treachery from the Tomar king Silhadi.

Akbar arranged matrimonial alliances to gain the trust of Rajput rulers. He himself married the Rajput princess Jodha Bai, the daughter of the Maharaja of Amer. He also granted high offices to a large number of Rajput princes and this maintained very cordial relations with them. Before long, these actions caused many previously hostile Rajputs to be his friends, and many of them surrendered their kingdoms to him. Rulers like Raja Maan Singh of Amer were trusted allies. However, some Rajput rulers were not ready to accept Akbar's dominance and preferred to remain independent. Two such rulers were

Rana Uday Singh of Mewar and Rao Chandrasen Rathore of Marwar. They never accepted Akbar's supremacy and were at constant war with him. This struggle was continued by – Rana Pratap. He fought a terrible battle with Akbar at the Haldighat pass where he was defeated and wounded. Since then Rana Pratap remained in recluse for 12 years and attacked the Mughal ruler from time to time. He fought valiantly throughout his life never ceded his independence to the Mughal ruler.

An ancient ruin in Jaisalmer, Rajasthan.

When Rajput rulers lost to invaders during the medieval period, their womenfolk would commit suicide by self-immolation on a pyre. This was a gesture to protect their chastity and self-respect, and it was known as Jauhar.

Rajasthan's formerly independent kingdoms created a rich architectural and cultural heritage, seen today in their numerous forts and palaces (Mahals and Havelis) which are enriched by features of Muslim and Jain architecture.

Maratha Empire

Since the early 1700s, the Maratha Empire began expanding

northwards, led by Peshwa Baji Rao I of Pune. This expansion finally brought the newly founded Hindu Maratha Empire in contact with the Rajputs. Rajasthan saw many invasions by the Marathas, under military leadership of Holkars and Scindhias. Most of Rajputana passed under the control of the Maratha Empire and continued to pay tribute to Pune till the British East India Company replaced the Marathas as paramount rulers.

British Rajasthan

The arrival of the British East India Company in the region led to the administrative designation of some geographically, culturally, economically and historically diverse areas, which had never shared a common political identity, under the name of the Rajputana Agency. This was a significant identifier, being modified later to Rajputana Province and lasting until the renaming to Rajasthan in 1949. The Company officially recognised various entities, although sources disagree concerning the details, and also included Ajmer-Merwara, which was the only area under direct British control. Of these various areas, Marwar and Jaipur were the most significant in the early 19th-century, although it was Mewar that gained particular attention from James Tod, a Company employee who was enamoured of Rajputana and wrote extensively, if often uncritically, of the people, history and geography of the Agency as a whole. Alliances were formed between the Company and these various princely and chiefly entities in the early 19th century, accepting British sovereignty in return for local autonomy and protection from the Marathas. Following the Mughal tradition and more importantly due to its strategic location Ajmer became a province of British India, while the autonomous Rajput states, the Muslim state Tonk (princely state), and the Jat states Bharatpur, [Dholpur] were organized into the Rajputana Agency. In 1817-18, the British Government concluded treaties of alliance with almost all the states of Rajputana. Thus began the British rule over Rajasthan, then called Rajputana.

Post independence

The name of Rajasthan was probably popularised by Tod and during his lifetime some people believed that he had coined it.Although he claimed that it was the classical name for the region, the term seems first to be documented in an inscription dating from 1708 and to have become popular by his time.

It took seven stages to form Rajasthan as defined today. In March 1948 the Matsya Union consisted of Alwar, Bharatpur, Dhaulpur and Karauli was formed. Also, in March 1948 Banswara, Bundi, Dungarpur, Jhalawar, Kishangarh, Kota, Pratapgarh, Shahpura and Tonk joined the Indian union and formed a part of Rajasthan. In April 1948 Udaipur joined the state and the Maharana of Udaipur was made Rajpramukh. Therefore in 1948 the merger of south and southeastern states was almost complete. Still retaining their independence from India were Jaipur and the desert kingdoms of Bikaner, Jodhpur and Jaisalmer. From a security point of view, it was vital to the new Indian Union to ensure that the desert kingdoms were integrated into the new nation. The princes finally agreed to sign the Instrument of Accession, and the kingdoms of Bikaner, Jodhpur, Jaisalmer and Jaipur were merged in March 1949. This time the Maharaja of Jaipur, Man Singh II was made the Rajpramukh of the state and Jaipur became its capital. Later in 1949, the United States of Matsya, comprising the former kingdoms of Bharatpur, Alwar, Karauli and Dholpur, was incorporated into Rajasthan. On January 26, 1950, 18 states of united Rajasthan merged with Sirohi to join the state leaving Abu and Dilwara to remain a part of Greater Bombay and now Gujarat.

In November 1956, under the provisions of the States Re-organisation Act, the erstwhile part 'C' state of Ajmer, Abu Road Taluka, former part of Sirohi princely state (which were merged in former Bombay), State and Sunel-Tappa region of the former Madhya Bharat merged with Rajasthan and Sirohi sub district of Jhalawar was transferred to Madhya Pradesh. Thus giving the existing boundary Rajasthan. Today with further reorganisation of the states of Uttar Pradesh, Madhya Pradesh and Bihar. Rajasthan has become the largest state of the Indian Republic.

The princes of the former kingdoms were constitutionally granted handsome remuneration in the form of privy purses and privileges to assist them in the discharge of their financial obligations. In 1970, Indira Gandhi, who was then the Prime Minister of India, commenced under-takings to discontinue the privy purses, which were abolished in 1971. Many of the former princes still continue to use the title of Maharaja, but the title has little power other than status symbol. Many of the Maharajas still hold their palaces and have converted them into profitable hotels, while some have made good in politics. The democratically elected Government runs the state with a chief minister as its executive head and the governor as the head of the state. Currently, including the new district of Pratapgarh, there are 33 districts, 105 sub-divisions, 37,889 villages, 241 tehsils and 222 towns in Rajasthan.

Gurumukh Nihal Singh was appointed as first governor of Rajasthan. Hiralal Shastri was the first nominated chief minister of the state, taking office on 7 April 1949. He was succeeded by two other nominated holders of the office before Tika Ram Paliwal became the first elected chief minister from 3 March 1951.

2

Culture and Society

CULTURE OF RAJASTHAN

Rajasthan has artistic and cultural traditions which reflect the ancient Indian way of life.

Rajasthan was also called Rajputana (the country of the Rajputs);

It is also a tourism destination with lots of tourist attractions and good tourist facilities. This historical state of India attracts tourists and vacationers with its rich culture, tradition, heritage, and monuments. It has also some sanctuaries & national parks.

More than 70% of Rajasthan is vegetarian, which makes it the most vegetarian state in India.

CULTURE

Rajasthan is culturally rich and has artistic and cultural traditions which reflect the ancient Indian way of life. There is rich and varied folk culturefrom villages which are often depicted as a symbol of the state. Highly cultivated classical music and dance with its own distinct style is part of the cultural tradition of Rajasthan. The music has songs that depict day-to-day relationships and chores, often focused around fetching water from wells or ponds.

Rajasthani cooking was influenced by both the war-like lifestyles of its inhabitants and the availability of ingredients in this arid region. Food that could last for several days and could be eaten without heating was preferred. The scarcity of water and fresh green vegetables have all had their effect on the cooking. It is known for its snacks like Bikaneri Bhujia. Other famous dishes include *bajre ki roti* (millet bread) and *lahsun ki chutney*(hot garlic paste), *mawa kachori* Mirchi Bada, Pyaaj Kachori and ghevar from Jodhpur, Alwar ka Mawa(Milk Cake), *Kadhi kachori* from Ajmer, *malpauas* from Pushkar, Daal kachori (Kota kachori) from Kota and rassgollas from Bikaner. Originating from the Marwar region of the state is the concept Marwari Bhojnalaya, or vegetarian restaurants, today found in many parts of India, which offer vegetarian food of the Marwari people.

"Up-down" dolls are found in the roadside shops of Jaisalmer.

Dal-Bati-Churma is very popular in Rajasthan. The traditional way to serve it is to first coarsely mash the Baati then pour pure Ghee on top of it. It is served with the daal (lentils) and spicy garlic chutney. Also served with Besan (gram flour) ki kadi. It is commonly served at all festivities, including religious occasions, wedding ceremonies, and birthday parties in Rajasthan. "Dal-

Baati-Churma", is a combination of three different food items — Daal (lentils), Baati and Churma (Sweet). It is a typical Rajasthani dish.

The Ghoomar dance from Jodhpur Marwar and Kalbeliya dance of Jaisalmer have gained international recognition. Folk music is a large part of Rajasthani culture. Kathputli, Bhopa, Chang, Teratali, Ghindr, Kachchhighori, and Tejaji are examples of traditional Rajasthani culture. Folk songs are commonly ballads which relate heroic deeds and love stories; and religious or devotional songs known as bhajans and banis which are often accompanied by musical instruments like dholak, sitar, and sarangi are also sung.

Traditional musical instruments of Rajasthan

Rajasthan is known for its traditional, colourful art. The block prints, tie and dye prints, Bagaru prints, Sanganer prints, and Zari embroidery are major export products from Rajasthan. Handicraft items like wooden furniture and crafts, carpets, and blue pottery are commonly found here. Shopping reflects the colourful culture, Rajasthani clothes have a lot of mirror work and embroidery. A Rajasthani traditional dress for females comprises an ankle-length skirt and a short top, also known as a *lehenga* or a *chaniya choli.* A piece of cloth is used to cover the head, both for protection from heat and maintenance of modesty. Rajasthani dresses are usually designed in bright colours like blue, yellow and orange.

The main religious festivals are Deepawali, Holi, Gangaur, Teej, Gogaji, Shri Devnarayan Jayanti, Makar Sankranti and Janmashtami, as the main religion is Hinduism. Rajasthan's desert festival is held once a year during winter. Dressed in costumes, the people of the desert dance and sing ballads. There are fairs with snake charmers, puppeteers, acrobats and folk performers. Camels play a role in this festival.

MUSIC AND DANCE

Highly cultivated classical music and dance with its own distinct style is part of the cultural tradition of Rajasthan. The music is uncomplicated and songs depict day-to-day relationships and chores, more often focused around fetching water from wells or ponds.

The Ghoomar dance from Jodhpur and Kalbeliya dance of Jaisalmer have gained international recognition. Folk music is a vital part of Rajasthani culture. Kathputali, Bhopa, Chang, Teratali, Ghindar, Kachchhighori, Tejaji,parth dance etc. are the examples of the traditional Rajasthani culture. Folk songs are commonly ballads which relate heroic deeds and love stories; and religious or devotional songs known as bhajans and banis (often accompanied by musical instruments like dholak, sitar, sarangi etc.) are also sung.

Kanhaiya Geet also sung in major areas of east rajasthani belt in the collectiong manner as a best source of entertainment in the rural areas.

Arts and crafts

Rajasthan is famous for textiles, semi-precious stones and handicrafts, and for its traditional and colorful art. Rajasthani furniture has intricate carvings and bright colours. Block prints, tie and dye prints, Bagaru prints, Sanganer prints and

Zariembroidery are major export products from Rajasthan. The blue pottery of Jaipur is particularly noted.

A carpet seller in Jaipur

Architecture

Rajasthan is famous for its many historical forts, temples and palaces (havelis), which predominantly drives tourism in the state.

Forts of Rajasthan

- Amber Fort, Jaipur

- Bala Qila, Alwar
- Barmer Fort, Barmer
- Chittorgarh Fort, Chittorgarh
- Gagron Fort, Jhalawar
- Gugor Fort, Baran
- Jaigarh Fort, Jaipur
- Jaisalmer Fort, Jaisalmer
- Jalore Fort, Jalore,
- Jhalawar Fort, Jhalawar
- Juna Fort and Temple, Barmer
- Junagarh Fort, Bikaner
- Khandhar Fort, Sawai Madhopur
- Khejarla Fort, Jodhpur
- Khimsar Fort, Nagaur
- Kumbhalgarh Fort, Rajsamand
- Lohagarh Fort, Bharatpur
- Mehrangarh Fort, Jodhpur
- Nagaur Fort, Nagaur
- Nahargarh Fort, Jaipur
- Nahargarh Fort, Baran
- Neemrana Fort Palace, Alwar
- Ranthambore Fort, Sawai Madhopur
- Taragarh Fort, Bundi
- Shergarh Fort, Baran
- Surajgarh Fort, Surajgarh

Palaces of Rajasthan

- Alwar City Palace, Alwar
- Amber Palace, Jaipur
- Badal Mahal, Dungarpur
- Dholpur Palace, Bharatpur
- Fateh Prakash Palace, Chittorgarh

- Gajner Palace and Lake, Bikaner
- Jag Mandir, Udaipur
- Jagmandir Palace, Kota
- Jaipur City Palace, Jaipur
- Jal Mahal, Jaipur
- Juna Mahal, Dungarpur
- Lake Palace, Udaipur
- Lalgarh Palace and Museum, Bikaner
- Laxmi Niwas Palace, Bikaner
- Man Mahal, Pushkar
- Mandir Palace, Jaisalmer
- Monsoon Palace, Udaipur
- Moti Doongri, Alwar
- Moti Doongri, Jaipur
- Moti Mahal, Jodhpur
- Nathmal Ji Ki Haveli, Jaisalmer
- Patwon Ki Haveli, Jaisalmer
- Phool Maha, Jodhpur
- Raj Mandir, Banswara
- Rampuria Haveli, Bikaner
- Rana Kumbha Palace, Chittorgarh
- Rani Padmini's Palace, Chittorgarh
- Ranisar Padamsar, Jodhpur
- Ratan Singh Palace, Chittorgarh
- Salim Singh Ki Haveli, Jaisalmer
- Sardar Samand Lake and Palace, Jodhpur
- Sheesh Mahal, Jodhpur
- Sisodia Rani Palace and Garden, Jaipur
- Sukh Mahal, Bundi
- Sunheri Kothi, Sawaimadhopur
- Udai Bilas Palace , Dungarpur
- Udaipur City Palace, Udaipur

- Umaid Bhawan Palace, Jodhpur

Religion

Rajasthan is home to all the major religions of India. Hindus are the largest in number, accounting for 87.45% of the population. Muslims (10.08%), Sikhs (1.27%), Jains (1%) and Sindhi's constitute the remaining of the population.

Festivals

The main religious festivals are Deepawali, Holi, Gangaur, Teej, Gogaji, Makar Sankranti and Janmashtami, as the main religion is Hinduism. Rajasthan's desert festival is celebrated with great zest and zeal. This festival is held once a year during winters. People of the desert dance and sing ballads of valor, romance and tragedy. There are fairs with snake charmers, puppeteers, acrobats and folk performers. Camels play a prominent role in this festival.

Religious syncretism

Rajasthan has several popular Hindu saints, many from the Bhakti era.

Rajasthani saints hail from all castes; Maharshi Naval Ram and Umaid Ram Maharaj were Bhangis, Karta Ram Maharaj was a Shudra, Sundardasa was a Vaish, and Meerabai and Ramdeoji were Rajputs. The backward caste Nayaks serve as the narrators or the devotional music (or "bhajan") for the Baba Ramdevji sect.

The most popular Hindu deities are Surya, Krishna and Rama.

Modern-day popular saints from Rajasthan have been Paramyogeshwar Sri Devpuriji of Kriya Yoga and Swami Satyananda the master of Kriya Yoga, Kundalini Yoga, Mantra Yoga and Laya yoga. Rajasthan had a massive movement to unite the Hindus and Muslims to worship God together. Saint Baba Ramdevji was adored by Muslims, equally that he was to Hindus.

Mostly Rajasthani speaks Marwari language.It is their native language.

Saint Dadu Dayal was a popular figure who came from Gujarat to Rajasthan to preach the unity of Ram and Allah. Sant Rajjab was a saint born in Rajasthan who became a disciple of Dadu Dayal and spread the philosophy of unity amongst Hindu and Muslim worshipers of God.

Saint Kabir was another popular figure noted for bringing the Hindu and Muslim communities together, and stressing that God may have many forms (e.g., whether in the form or Rama or Allah.)

3

Government and Politics

GOVERNMENT OF RAJASTHAN

The Government of Rajasthan also known as the State Government of Rajasthan, or locally as State Government, is the supreme governing authority of the Indian state of Rajasthan and its 33 districts. It consists of an executive, led by the Governor of Rajasthan, a judiciary and a legislative. Jaipur is the capital of Rajasthan, and houses the Vidhan Sabha(Legislative Assembly) and the secretariat.

State Government

Like other states in India, the head of state of Rajasthan is the Governor, appointed by the President of India on the advice of the Central government. His or her post is largely ceremonial. The Chief Minister is the head of government and is vested with most of the executive powers.

Legislature

The present Legislature of Rajasthan is unicameral, consisting of Legislative Assembly, which consists of 200 M.L.A.. The assembly sits for terms of a maximum of 5 years.

Judiciary

The Rajasthan High Court is having its principal seat in Jodhpur, and a bench at Jaipur which have respective jurisdiction over the neighboring districts of Rajasthan.

Local Governments

Local governments consists of Panchayati Raj Institutions(PRIs) for rural areas and Municipalities or Urban Local Bodies(ULBs) for urban areas.

GOVERNMENT AND POLITICS

The politics of Rajasthan is dominated mainly by the Bharatiya Janata Party and the Indian National Congress. The Chief Minister, serving the second term, is Vasundhara Raje.

Administrative divisions

The Jain temple at Ranakpur is in Pali district.

RAJASTHAN LEGISLATIVE ASSEMBLY

The Rajasthan Legislative Assembly or the Rajasthan

Vidhan Sabha is the unicameral legislature of the Indianstate of Rajasthan. The assembly meets at Vidhana Bhavan situated in Jaipur, the capital of Rajasthan. Members of the Legislative assembly are directly elected by the people for a term of 5 years. Presently, the legislative assembly consists of 200 members.

History

The First Rajasthan Legislative Assembly (1952–57) was inaugurated on 31 March 1952. It had a strength of 160 members. The strength was increased to 190 after the merger of the erstwhile Ajmer State with Rajasthan in 1956. The Second (1957–62) and Third (1962–67) Legislative Assemblies had a strength of 176. The Fourth (1967–72) and Fifth (1972–77) Legislative Assembly comprised 184 members each. The strength became 200 from the Sixth (1977–80) Legislative Assembly onwards. The Fourteenth Legislative Assembly was commenced on 21 January 2013. Umed Singh of Barmer was youngest member of Rajasthan Legislative Assembly, as in 1962 election Result was declared on 19 February 1962 and he was elected from Barmer, that time he was just 25 year and 4 months old.

POLITICS OF RAJASTHAN

Politics of Rajasthan is dominated by two parties Bharatiya Janata Party (BJP) and Indian National Congress. The current government in Rajasthan is that of Bharatiya Janata Party. The Chief Minister is Vasundhara Raje.

Rajasthan's politics has mainly been dominated by the two state stalwarts, namely, Bhairon Singh Shekhawat and Mohan Lal Sukhadia of the Bharatiya Janata Partyand the Indian National Congress respectively. Shri Sukhadia ruled Rajasthan for 17 years and died in February 1982 while Late Shri Shekhawat was in the national political horizon. The earlier politics were dominated by the Congress party. The main opposition party was the Bharatiya Jansangh, headed by Rajasthan's most popular leader Bhairon Singh Shekhawat and the Swatantra party headed by former rulers of Rajasthan. The Congress rule was untouched till the year 1962. But in 1967, Jansangh headed by Shekhawat and Swatantra party headed by Rajmata Gayatri Devi of Jaipur reached the majority point, but couldn't form a government. In 1972, the Congress won a landslide victory following the victory in the 1971 war. But after the declaration of emergency, Shekhawat became immensely popular, especially after he was forced to be arrested and was sent to Rohtak Jail in Haryana. As soon as the emergency was lifted, a joint opposition Janta Party won a thundering landslide victory winning 151 of the 200 seats. Shekhawat became the Chief Minister. The government was dismissed by Indira Gandhi in 1980 after she restored power in Delhi. In the 1980 elections, the Janta Party split at the centre giving the Congress a victory in Rajasthan.

Indira Gandhi was assassinated in 1984, and in 1985, a sympathy wave let the Congress sail through in the elections. But in 1989, which could be called a Shekhawat wave, the BJP-JD alliance won all 25 Lok Sabha seats and 140 of 200 seats in the assembly. Shekhawat became the Chief Minister for the second term. Though Janta Dal took back its support to the Shekhawat government, Shekhawat tore apart the JD and continued to rule as the Chief Minister thus earning the title of master manipulator. After the Babri Mosque demolition in Ayodhya, Shekhawat government was suspended by the P.M., Narsimha Rao and President's rule was enforced in Rajasthan. Election took place in 1993 in which his party won even after the breaking of its alliance with the Janta Dal. But the then governor Bali Ram Bhagat didn't allow Shekhawat to form the government, but after immense pressure from Shekhawat, who reached the majority point after supports from independents like Sardar Gurjant Singh, Rani Narendra Kanwar, Sujan Singh Yadav, Rohitashva Kumar Sharma, Kr. Arun Singh, Sundar Lal etc. crossed the majority line of 101 seats in the assembly. Shekhawat became the Chief Minister for the third term. This time he ran a successful third term. This was perhaps the diamond phase for Rajasthan as it led to all-round development and Rajasthan also gained identity on the globe as a rapidly developing and beautiful state.Shekhawat introduced Heritage, Desert, Rural, Wildlife tourism to Rajasthan In 1998 elections, the BJP lost heavily due to the onion price rise issue. Ashok Gehlot ran a 5-year government. But he lost the Lok Sabha elections in 1999, only 6 months after its victory in the assembly elections. Shekhawat became the Vice-President of India in 2002 so he had to leave Rajasthan politics and the BJP. He appointed Vasundhara Raje as his successor. She led the BJP in 2003 elections and led it to a victory. She was the Chief Minister of Rajasthan from 2003 - 2008. Narpat Singh Rajvi was the Health Minister, Ghanshyam Tiwari was the Food Minister, and Gulab Chand Kataria was the Home Minister. The BJP won the 2004 Lok Sabha elections from here as well. But the tables turned in December 2008, when the infighting within the BJP, Raje's perceived autocratic and despotic rule, and the police excesses in the Gurjar-Meena agitation combined to overcome the incumbent Raje government's development and growth planks, and the Congress emerged victorious with the support of some independent MLA's. Ashok Gehlot was sworn-in as the new Chief Minister of Rajasthan. In 2013 Bharatiya Janata Party won by very large difference. BJP got 163 seats and Congress got only 21 seats out of 200 seats. Vasundhara Raje became the Chief Minister for second time.

4

Language and Literature

LANGUAGES OF RAJASTHAN

The primarily spoken language of Rajasthan is Hindi. However, when the state of Rajasthan was founded, a number of princely states were merged. This led to the emergence of different dialects in the local languages of Rajasthan.

The four main dialects of Rajasthani language are:

Marwari

The Marwari dialect is mainly spoken in the western Rajasthan. In fact, Marwari is the most widely spoken dialect in Rajasthan.

Jaipuri/Dhundhari

In the east and southeast regions of Rajasthan, the Jaipuri dialect is spoken. Also known as Dhundhari, this dialect forms is spoken by the maximum number of Rajasthanis, after Marwari.

Malvi/Malwi

The people of the southeast region speak in the Malvi (Malwi) dialect, apart from Jaipuri. This dialect covers the Malwa tract i.e., Indore, Bhopal, Mandsor and the Ujjain area.

Mewati

In Alwar and the surrounding region, Mewati dialect is heavily used. It is somewhat like the Braj bhasha spoken in Bharatpur district.

Apart from these major dialects, a number of other dialects are also spoken in Rajasthan. Some of these are Harauti, Kishangarhi and so on. However, English is also widely understood in Rajasthan. You also get guides and translators in Rajasthan speaking foreign languages like German, French, Chinese, Japanese, etc.

FAMOUS LANGUAGES AND LITERATURES IN RAJASTHAN

The language of Rajasthan is Rajasthani which consists of five principal dialects like Marwari, Dhundhari, Mewari, Mewati and Hadauti. It is derived from Apabhramsa, with all its linguistic and orthographical peculiarities.

Rajasthani as a language of literature suffered a great set back during the British period. Today hundreds of poets and writers are writing in Rajasthani. Folk literature in Rajasthani is varied and rich and consists of songs, tales, sayings, riddles and folk-plays popularly known as khyals.

Marwari: Rajasthani is divided into four big groups, the biggest being that of Marwari. Standard Marwari is spoken mainly in and around Jodhpur district and has some influence on the dialects in Barmer, Jalore, Pali and part of Nagaur district. The dialect is also spoken in mixed form in the east in Ajmer, Udaipur, Bhilwara and Chittorgarh district; in the south in Sirohi district and the Palanpur district of Gujarat; in the west in Jaisalmer district and in the north in Bikaner, Churu, Sikar and Jhunjhunu districts. It is also spoken with some Punjabi influence in Ganganagar district in the north-west. In the south-east in Mewar (Udaipur, Bhilwara and

Chittorgarh districts) and its neighbourhood, there is the well-known eastern form of Marwari known as Mewari.

In the southern part of Pali and Jalore districts, the whole of Sirohi district and the northern part of Palanpur, there is a southern sub-dialect. The dialect spoken in the western parts of Barmer, Jaisalmer, Thar and Parkar areas of Sind is called Thali in the north and Dhatak in the west.

Northern forms of Marwari cover Bikaner, Churu, Ganganagar, Sikar and Jhunjhunu districts. In Bikaner it is called Bikaneri while in the north-eastern part of Churu it is known as Bagri.

Dhundhari: The second big group of Rajasthani is formed by eastern Rajasthani or Jaipuri, better known as Dhundhari. It covers the districts of Jaipur, Tonk, Kota and Bundi and parts of Kishangarh, Ajmer and Jhalawar. In the north-east, Eastern Rajasthani has the Mewati dialect of the same language, while further east, from north to south, it is Braja Bhasha in Bharatpur, the Dang sub-dialect of Braja Bhasa in Sawai-Madhopur and Karauli, Bundeli and Malvi in Jhalawar and the southern parts of Kota.

Harauti: Kishangarhi is spoken in the whole of the Kishangarh sub-division and in a small belt to the north of Ajmer and Ajmeri is spoken over the eastern centre of Ajmer district. The dialect of Bundi and Kota is Harauti, which is also spoken in the neighbouring parts of the Jhalwar and Tonk districts and the Gwalior district of Madhya Pradesh. In the latter region it is known as Sheopuri.

Mewati is the language of Mewat, the abode of the Meos, but it covers a larger tract than that which sprawls over the north-west of the Bharatpur and Alwar districts. It is also spoken in the south east of Haryana in Gurgaon district and in the Kot-Kasin area of Jaipur. It represents a Rajasthani dialect fading off into the Bangru dialect of Hindi.

Malvi: Malvi is spoken in the Malwa tract *i.e.*, Indore. Bhopal, Mandsor and the Ujjain area. In the east, it extends to the parts of the Jhalawar and Kota districts. In the north,

Malvi has the east-central dialect of Rajasthani of which Jaipuri has been taken as the standard. To the east, it has the Bundeli dialect of western Hindi spoken in Gwalior and Sagar.

In the south, it has from east to west, the Bundeli of Narsinghpur and central Hoshangabad, the Marathi of Berar and the Nemadi dialect of Rajasthani spoken in north Nimach and Bhansawar. To its north-west, it has the Mewari form of Marwari and Gujrathi and in the south-west Khandesi. Malvi is distinctly Rajasthani dialect having relations with Marwari and Jaipuri (Dhundhari).

The Bhils have a separate dialect, Bhili, spoken from the south of Merwara in the Aravali range in Udaipur district and further south in the districts of Dungarpur and Banswara. The dialect if Dungarpur, Banswara, is a Bagria form of Rajasthani, which the Bhils also speak with slight variation. The only difference is that of pronunciation but the structure of the language is the same.

Marwari and Dhundhari are large groups of local dialects within Rajasthan while Malvi has an outside origin. Bagri and Mewati are small groups within the state. Each of these groups consists of so many sub-dialects with so many local names. On the outskirts of their respective areas these dialects also show the marked influence of Braj, Labanda, Sindhi, Bundeli, Bangru, Gujarati and Punjabi or their dialects in the adjoining tracts.

Bagri Language

Bagri is a transitional dialect of Rajasthani language of the Indo-Aryan family. In India for political reasons it is tagged together with Bangru, a dialect of Rajasthani language which is considered a hindi variant and is spoken in the area adjacent to Bagri.

It is spoken by about five million speakers in Hanumangarh and Sriganganagar districts of Rajasthan, Sirsa and Hissar districts of Haryana, Firozepur and Muktsar districts of Punjab of India and Bahawalpur and Bahawalnagar areas of Punjab of Pakistan. Bagri is a typical Indo-Aryan language having

SOV word order. The most prominent phonological feature of Bagri is the presence of three lexical tones: high, level, and low.

Bhil Languages

The Bhil languages are a group of Central Indo-Aryan languages spoken by some 6 million Bhils in western, central, and by small numbers, even in far eastern, India. They constitute the primary languages of the southern Aravali Range in Rajasthan and the western Satpura Range in Madhya Pradesh.

Relationship

The Bhil languages form a link midway between the Gujarati language and the Rajasthani languages.

The group is comprised of the following languages:

- Adiwasa Garasia language
- Bareli language
- Bauria language
- Bhilali language
- Bhili language
- Bhilori language
- Chodri language
- Dhodia language
- Dubli language
- Dungra Bhil language
- Gamit language
- Mawchi language
- Pardhi language
- Rajput Garasia language
- Rathawi language
- Wagdi language

Dhatki Language

Dhatki, also known as Dhati or Thari, is a sociolect of Marwari dialect of Rajasthani language. It is spoken in western parts of Jaisalmer and Barmer districts of Rajasthan in India and eastern parts of Sindh province of Pakistan. It's characteristic phonological features are glottalized or implosive sounds. Many Dhatki speaking communities migrated to India in 1947 after the partition and continued thereafter in small numbers, but still there is a sizeable number of Dhatki speakers in Pakistan. Few of the typical sentences in Dhatki are: 1. "Ki karinto" meaning "what are you doing", 2. "Tayo naam ki hai" meaning "what is your name, 3. "maaye roti khaani hai" meaning "i need to eat".

Dhundari Language

Dhundari is an Indo-Aryan language spoken in the Dhundhar region of northeastern Rajasthan state, India. Dhundari-speaking people are found in three districts - Jaipur, Dausa, and Tonk. The derivation of the name "Dhundari" is thought to be from two origins.

According to the first opinion, Dhundari is believed to have drawn its name from the Dhundh or Dhundhakriti mountain, which is situated near Jobner in Jaipur District. The other opinion is that it is named after a river called Dhundh flowing through this region. Hence the name became Dhundhar.

According to the 1991 census, the total population of Dhundari speakers is 965,008.

Dhundari is classified as Indo-European, Indo-Iranian, Indo-Aryan, Central Zone, Rajasthani, Marwari. Alternative names for Dhundari are Dhundhali, Dhundhahdi, Jhadshahi boli, and Kai-kui boli and Jaipuri. Jaipuri was coined by the European scholars such as Mac Alister and Grierson Abraham. Ethnologue adds Dhundari-Marwari (Gordon 2005) to this language.

Mac Alister completed the grammatical analysis in February 24, 1884. Books such as Moksha Marga Prakashak have been written in Dhundari by Acharyakalpa Pt. Todarmalji on Jain philosophy.

The Serampore missionaries translated the New Testament into Jaipuri proper in 1815. It is not known whether there are any extant copies of the New Testament translation. The sentence structure is SOV. No systematic language development is carried out in this language

Dingal

Dingal is an Ancient Indian language written in Nagri script and having literature in Prose as well as poetry.

Goaria Language

Goaria is a Rajasthani language spoken by some 25,000 people in Sindh Province,.

Godwari

Godwari is a dialect of Marwari spoken in Godwar.

Harauti Language

The Harauti language is a dialect of Rajasthani language of Indo-Aryan language family. It is spoken in Kota, Baran, Bundi and Jhalawar districts of Rajasthan and its adjacent areas of Madhya Pradesh. Its word order is typical Subject Object Verb (SOV) and its characteristic feature, unlike Hindi, is presence or absence of agentive marker in perfect tense depending on the nature of accusative marker.

Jaipuri

Jaipuri language refers to the dialect of the Rajasthani language spoken in the Indian state of Rajasthan, in and around the Jaipur region. It is often regarded as a dialect of Hindi.

Malvi Language

Malvi is the language of the Malwa region of India, with more than a million speakers. The language is also sometimes known as Malavi, Ujjaini, etc. Malvi is classified with the Rajasthani languages, with Nimadi, spoken in the Nimar region of Madhya Pradesh and in Rajasthan, being its closest cousin. The dialects of Malvi are, in alphabetical order, Bachadi, Bhoyari, Dholewari, Hoshangabadi, Jamral, Katiyai, Malvi

Proper, Patvi, Rangari, Rangri and Sondwari. A survey in 2001 found only 4 dialects: Ujjaini (Ujjain, Indore, Dewas, Sehore districts), Rajawadi (Ratlam, Mandsaur, Neemuch districts), Umadwadi (Rajgarh district) and Sondhwadi (Jhalawar District, Rajasthan). About 55% of the population of Malwa can converse in Hindi, which is the official language of the Madhya Pradesh state, and literacy rate in second language (Hindi) is about 40%.

Marwari Language

The Marwari language (also variously Marvari, Marwadi, Marvadi) is spoken in the Indian state of Rajasthan, but is also found in the neighbouring state of Gujarat and in Eastern Pakistan. With some 13.2 million speakers (as of 1997, ca. 13 million in India and 200,000 in Pakistan) it is the largest of the Marwari subgroup of the "Rajasthani cluster" of western dialects of Hindi. It is written with the Devanagari script, as is Hindi. Marwari currently has no official status as a language of education and government. There has been a push in the recent past for the national government to recognize this language and give it a scheduled status. The state of Rajasthan recognizes Rajasthani as a language. Some consider Rajasthani and Marwari to be the same language.

In Pakistan, there are two varieties of Marwari. They may or may not be close enough to Indian Marwari to be considered the same language.

The Marwari language was used in the recent Indian movie, Paheli, where it was mixed with Hindi so it is understandable to the main stream audience. Marwari is still spoken widely in and around Jodhpur. Closely related languages to Marwari in the Rajasthani cluster are: Shekhawati, Hadoti, Dundhari, Mewari, Brij, Bagri, Wagri, Mewati, and others. There are ongoing efforts to identify and classify this language cluster and the language differences.

CLASSIFICATION AND RELATED LANGUAGES

Geographical Distribution: Dark green indicates Marwari speaking home area in Rajasthan, light green indicates additional dialect areas where speakers identify their language as Marwari. Marwari is primarily spoken in the Indian state of Rajasthan. Marwari speakers have dispersed widly through out India and other countries but are found most notably in the neighbouring state of Gujarat and in Eastern Pakistan. With some 13.2 million speakers (as of 1997, ca. 13 million in India and 200,000 in Pakistan) it is the largest of the Marwari subgroup of the "Rajasthani cluster" of western dialects of Hindi.

Phonology

It shares a 50%-65% lexical similarity with Hindi (this is based on a Swadesh 210 word list comparison). Marwari has many cognate words with Hindi. Notable phonetic correspondences include /s/ in Hindi with /h/ in Marwari. For example /sona/ 'gold' (Hindi) and /hono/ 'gold' (Marwari). /h/ sometimes elides. There are also a variety of vowel changes. Most of the pronouns and interrogatives are, however, distinct from those of Hindi.

Grammar: Marwari has a very similar grammar to that of Hindi. Its primary sentence structure is SOV (Subject, Object, Verb).

VOCABULARY

Writing System: Marwari had two scripts before the present devanagri script. The script presently is a modified form of the one used for Hindi with the most notable difference being the addition of a retroflex lateral "?". This character is found in sanscrict but not in Hindi. Some publications in Marwari also use some other characters in substitution for accepted letters.

Marwari Languages: The Marwari languages are a subgroup of the "Rajasthani language" of Hindi dialects. They include Marwari proper (13.2 million speakers) as well as Dhundari (9 million), Shekhawati (3 million), Mewari (1 million), Dhatki (130,000), Goaria (25,000), Loarki (20,000), Mewati (1,300) and Godwari.

Mewari Language: Mewari is one of the major dialects of Rajasthani language of Indo-Aryan languages family. It is spoken by about five million speakers in Rajsamand, Bhilwara, Udaipur, and Chittorgarh districts of Rajasthan state of India. It has SOV word order. There are 31 consonants, 10 vowels, and 2 diphthongs in Mewari. Intonation is prominent. Dental fricative is replaced by glottal stop at initial and medial positions. Inflection and derivation are the forms of word formation. There are two numbers—singular and plural, two genders--masculine and feminine, and three cases--simple, oblique, and vocative. Case marking is partly inflectional and partly postpositional. Concord is of subject-verb type. Nouns are declined according to their endings. Pronouns are inflected for number, person, and gender. There are three tenses--present, past, and future; and four moods. Adjective are of two types--either ending in /-o/ or not ending in /-o/. Three participles are there--present, past, and prefect.

Mewati: Mewati, a dialect of Rajasthani language of Indo-Aryan family, is spoken by about five million speakers in Alwar, Bharatpur and Dholpur districts of Rajasthan, and Faridabad and Gurgaon districts of Haryana states of India. Extensive linguistic research work has not carried out on this dialect so far. It had contributed profoundly to Rajasthani literature in medieval periods.

There are 9 vowels, 31 consonants, and 2 diphthongs. Suprasegmentals are not so prominent as they are in the other dialects of Rajasthani. There are two numbers--singular and plural, two genders--masculine and feminine; and three cases--direct, oblique, and vocative.

The nouns decline according to their final segments. Case marking is postpositional. Pronouns are traditional in nature and are inflected for number and case. Gender is not distinguished in pronouns. Two types of adjectives are there. There are three tenses--past, present, and future. Participles function as adjectives.

Rajasthani Language: Rajasthani is one of the prominent members of Indo-Aryan languages family. It is spoken by around eighty million persons (total number of speakers 36 million as per Census of India, 2001) in Rajasthan and other states of India, and has eight major dialects: Bagri, Shekhawati, Mewati, Dhundhari, Harauti, Marwari, Mewari, and Wagri.

Most of these dialects of Rajasthani are chiefly spoken in the state of Rajasthan but also in Gujarat, Haryana and Punjab. Besides, Rajasthani is spoken in some parts of western Madhya Pradesh, and the Pakistani provinces of Punjab and Sind.

Rajasthani language is classified in the Central Zone of the Indo-Aryan languages, which also includes Hindi and Urdu. Some of the dialects of Rajasthani are considered by some to be dialects of Hindi; however, many linguists agree that Rajasthani is a different language from Hindi at phonological, morphological, syntactical and lexical levels.

DIALECTS

Some major dialects of Rajasthani are:

- Bagri
- Shekhawati
- Mewati
- Marwari
- Dhundhari
- Harauti
- Mewari
- Wagri or Bhili

Some of the recognized minor dialects of Rajasthani are (last two are questionable in this category):

- Dhatki
- Goaria
- Loarki
- Gade Lohar
- Thali
- Sansiboli
- Romany

- Gujari or Gojari
- Malvi
- Nimadi

LITERATURE

Rajasthani has a vast literature written in various genres starting from 1000 AD. In the past, the language spoken in Rajasthan was regarded as a dialect of western Hindi (Kellogg, 1873). George Abraham Grierson (1908) was the first scholar who gave the designation 'Rajasthani' to the language, which was earlier known through its various dialects. Today, however, Sahitya Akademi, National Academy of Letters and University Grants Commission recognize it as a distinct language. It is also taught as such in the Universities of Jodhpur and Udaipur. The Board of Secondary Education, Rajasthan included Rajasthani in the course of studies and it has been an optional subject since 1973. Since 1947, several movements have been going on in Rajasthan for its recognition, but unfortunately it is still considered a 'dialect' of Hindi. Recently, the Rajasthan Government has recognized it as a state language, but still, there is a long way for Rajasthani language to go. The reason is it lacks a comprehensive reference grammar and latest dictionary prepared based on a thorough linguistic survey of Rajasthan. Now an extensive descriptive grammar of Rajasthani is under process.

Prominent Rajasthani Linguists

- Abdul Vaheed `Kamal'
- George Mac Alister
- George Abraham Grierson
- Ram Karan Asopa
- L. P. Tessitory
- Suniti Kumar Chatterjee
- Sita Ram Lalas
- Narottam Das Swami

- Kali Charan Bahl
- David Magier
- John D Smith
- Liudmila Khokhlova
- Peter E. Hook
- Anvita Abbi
- Lakhan gusain

Eminent Rajasthani Literateurs

- List of winners of Sahitya Akademi Awards for writing in Rajasthani language
- Chander Singh "Birkali"
- Kiran Nahta
- Nathuram Sanskrita
- Surajmal Mishran
- Narayan Singh Bhatti
- Kanhaiya Lal Sethia
- Kripa Ram Puniya
- Bastigiri Gusain
- Rani Lakshmi Kumari Chundawat
- Vijay Dan Detha
- Nanuram Sanskrita
- Shanti Bhardwaj "Rakesh"
- Shakidan Kaviya
- Kanhaiya Lal Dugar

Sansiboli

Sansiboli is a highly endangered dialect of Rajasthani language of Indo-Aryan family. It is spoken by about sixty thousand speakers mainly in Rajasthan, Haryana, Punjab, and Delhi states of India. As a language, Sansiboli is not confined to any particular geographical boundary. It has benefited from various sources, absorbed regional colours, and imbibed influence from neighbouring languages and dialects. Thus, it has numerous phonological and morphological borrowings from Punjabi, Hindi, and Gujarati.

Sansiboli is not effectively being passed on to the next generation and is on the verge of extinction. Very few people below the age of forty are fully competent in the language, and probably none of them will become active speakers. Many of the Sansis are likely to mix Hindi, Punjabi, or Gujarati elements in their speech depending on their geographical location.

Shekhawati Language

Shekhawati is a dialect of Rajasthani language of Indo-Aryan languages family and is spoken by about three million speakers in Churu, Jhunjhunu and Sikar districts of Rajasthan. Though a very important dialect from the grammatical and literary points of view, yet very little work is carried out on it. In 2001 A descriptive grammar of Shekhawati has been published. Shekhawati, like Bagri dialect of Ganganagar and Hanumangarh districts, has parallel lexicon which make it very rich from the lexicographical point of view. Word order is typical SOV and there is existence of implosives. Beside presence of high tone at suprasegmental level classify it with other dialects of Rajasthani. It has contributed a lot to the development of Rajasthani language and linguistics.

5

Geography and Flora & Fauna

GEOGRAPHY

The geographic features of Rajasthan are the Thar Desert and the Aravalli Range, which runs through the state from southwest to northeast, almost from one end to the other, for more than 850 kilometres (530 mi). Mount Abu lies at the southwestern end of the range, separated from the main ranges by the West Banas River, although a series of broken ridges continues into Haryana in the direction of Delhi where it can be seen as outcrops in the form of the Raisina Hill and the ridges farther north. About three-fifths of Rajasthan lies northwest of the Aravallis, leaving two-fifths on the east and south direction.

The northwestern portion of Rajasthan is generally sandy and dry. Most of this region is covered by the Thar Desert which extends into adjoining portions of Pakistan. The Aravalli Range does not intercept the moisture-giving southwest monsoon winds off the Arabian Sea, as it lies in a direction parallel to that of the coming monsoon winds, leaving the northwestern region in a rain shadow. The Thar Desert is thinly populated; the town of Jodhpur is the largest city in the desert and known as the gateway of thar desert. The desert has some major districts like

Jodhpur, Jaisalmer, Barmer, Bikaner and Nagour. This area is also important defence point of view. Jodhpur airbase is Indias largest airbase and military, BSF bases are also situated here. A single civil airport is also situated in Jodhpur.

Camel ride in the Thar Desert near Jaisalmer

The Northwestern thorn scrub forestslie in a band around the Thar Desert, between the desert and the Aravallis. This region receives less than 400 mm of rain in an average year. Temperatures can sometimes exceed 54 °C in the summer months or 129 degrees Fahrenheit and drop below freezing in the winter. The Godwar, Marwar, and Shekhawati regions lie in the thorn scrub forest zone, along with the city of Jodhpur. The Luni River and its tributaries are the major river system of Godwar and Marwar regions, draining the western slopes of the Aravallis and emptying southwest into the great Rann of Kutch wetland in neighbouring Gujarat.

This river is saline in the lower reaches and remains potable only up to Balotara in Barmer district. The Ghaggar River, which originates in Haryana, is an intermittent stream that disappears into the sands of the Thar Desert in the northern corner of the state and is seen as a remnant of the primitive Sarasvati river.

The Aravalli Range and the lands to the east and southeast of the range are generally more fertile and better watered. This region is home to the Kathiawar-Gir dry deciduous forestsecoregion, with tropical dry broadleaf forests that include teak, *Acacia*, and other trees. The hilly Vagad region, home to the cities of Dungarpur and Banswara lies in southernmost Rajasthan, on the border with Gujarat and Madhya Pradesh. With the exception of Mount Abu, Vagad is the wettest region in Rajasthan, and the most heavily forested. North of Vagad lies the Mewar region, home to the cities of Udaipur and Chittaurgarh. The Hadoti region lies to the southeast, on the border with Madhya Pradesh. North of Hadoti and Mewar lies the Dhundhar region, home to the state capital of Jaipur. Mewat, the easternmost region of Rajasthan, borders Haryana and Uttar Pradesh. Eastern and southeastern Rajasthan is drained by the Banas and Chambal rivers, tributaries of the Ganges.

Hills around Jaipur, viewed from Jaigarh Fort.

The Aravalli Range runs across the state from the southwest peak Guru Shikhar (Mount Abu), which is 1,722 metres (5,650 ft) in height, to Khetri in the northeast. This range divides the state into 60% in the northwest of the range and 40% in the southeast. The northwest tract is sandy and unproductive with little water but improves gradually from desert land in the far west and northwest to comparatively fertile and habitable land towards the east. The area includes the Thar Desert. The south-eastern area, higher in elevation (100 to 350 m above sea level) and more fertile, has a very diversified topography. in the south lies the hilly tract of Mewar. In the southeast, a large area within the districts of Kota and Bundi forms a tableland. To the northeast of these districts is a rugged region (badlands) following the line of the Chambal River. Farther north the country levels out; the flat plains of the northeastern Bharatpur district are part of an alluvial basin. Merta City lies in the geographical centre of Rajasthan.

TOPOGRAPHY

The Aravali Range runs across the state from the southwest peak Guru Shikhar (Mount Abu), which is 1,722 m in height to Khetri in the northeast. This divides the state into 60% in the northwest of the lines and 40% in the southeast. The northwest tract is sandy and unproductive with little water but improves gradually from desert land in the far west and northwest to comparatively fertile and habitable land towards the east. The area includes the Thar (Great Indian) Desert.

The south-eastern area, higher in elevation (100 to 350 m above sea level) and more fertile, has a very diversified topography in the south lies the hilly tract of Mewar. In the southeast, a large area of the districts of Kota and Bundi forms a tableland and to the northeast of these districts is a rugged region (badlands) following the line of the Chambal River. Farther north the country levels out; the flat plains of the northeastern Bharatpur district are part of the alluvial basin of the Yamuna River.

LOCATION OF RAJASTHAN IN INDIA

Rajasthan is located in the northwestern part of the subcontinent. It is bounded on the west and northwest by Pakistan, on the north and northeast by the states of Punjab, Haryana, and Uttar Pradesh, on the east and southeast by the states of Uttar Pradesh and Madhya Pradesh, and on the southwest by the state of Gujarat. The Tropic of Cancer passes through its southern tip in the Banswara district. The state has an area of 132,140 square miles (342,239 square kilometres). The capital city is Jaipur.

In the west, Rajasthan is relatively dry and infertile; this area includes some of the Thar Desert, also known as the Great Indian Desert. In the southwestern part of the state, the land is wetter, hilly, and more fertile.

The climate varies throughout Rajasthan. On average winter temperatures range from 8° to 28° C (46° to 82° F) and summer temperatures range from 25° to 46° C (77° to 115° F). Average rainfall also varies; the western deserts accumulate about 100 mm (about 4 in) annually, while the southeastern part of the state receives 650 mm (26 in) annually, most of which falls from July through September during the monsoon season. Rajasthan has a single-chamber legislative assembly with 200 seats. The state sends 35 members to the Indian national parliament: 10 to the Rajya Sabha (Upper House) and 25 to the Lok Sabha (Lower House). Local government is based on 30 administrative districts.

HINDU LUNAR MONTHS

The months of the Hindus lunar calendar (Vikram Samvat) and their Gregorian equivalents are as follows:

Chaitra	March-April
Vaishaka	Aril-May
Jyaistha	May-June
Asodha	June-July
Sravana	July-August

Bhadra	August-September
Asvina	September-October
Kartika	October-November
Aghan	November-December
Pausa	December-January
Magha	January-February
Phalguna	February-March

RAJASTHAN CLIMATE

The climate of Rajasthan can be divided into four seasons: Pre-Monsoons, Monsoon, Post-Monsoon and Winter.

Pre-monsoon, which extends from April to June, is the hottest season, with temperatures ranging from 32°C to 45°C. In western Rajasthan the temp may rise to 48C, particularly in May and June. At this time, Rajasthan only hill station, Mt Abu registers the lowest temperatures.

In the desert regions, the temperatures drops in night. Prevailing winds are from the west and sometimes carry dust storms (we call them andhi).

The second season Monsoon extends from July to September, temp drops but humidity increases making it very un comfortable, even when there is slight drop in the temp (35°C to 40°C). We have about 90% of our rains in this period.

The Post-monsoon period is from Oct to December. The average maximum temperature is 33°C to 38°C, and the minimum is between 18°C and 20°C.

The fourth season is the winter or cold season, from January to March. There is a marked variation in maximum and minimum temperatures, and regional variations across the state. January is the coolest month of the year. And temp may drop to 0°C in some cities of Rajasthan, like Churu. There is slight precipitation in the north and north-eastern region of the state, and light winds, predominantly from the north and north-east. At this time, relative humidity ranges from 50% to 60% in the morning, and 25% to 35% in the afternoon.

DISTRICTS OF RAJASTHAN

Ajmer; Bikaner; Dausa; Jhalawar; Pali; Tonk; Alwar; Bharatpur; Dungarpur; Jhunjhunu; Rajasmand; Udaipur; Banswara; Bundi; Hanumangarh; Jodhpur; Sawai Madohpur; Baran; Chittaurgarh; Jaipur; Karauli; Sikar; Barmer; Churu; Jaisalmer; Kota; Sirohi; Bhilwara; Dhaulpur; Jalor; Nagaur; Sri Ganganagar.

RANTHAMBORE NATIONAL PARK

Ranthambore National Park is located near the town of Sawai Madhopur, beautifully nestled between the Aravali and Vindhya mountain ranges. The park is rated among the most important and famous tiger reserves of India and it was among the first tiger reserves to be covered under the project tiger plan started in 1973 to protect tigers in India. Ranthambore National Park was declared a national park in the year 1980. Well spread in an area of 392 sq km; the park is home to a varied and rich wildlife including famous Royal Bengal Tigers. What makes this park more attractive is its picturesque topographical location. The Chambal River in the south and the Banas River in the north and six artificial lakes flowing through the park add to the beauty of the park. You can spot herds of wild animals along the banks of the rivers and lakes.

The Park houses about 30 mammals species, 275 bird species, 12 reptile species and 350 plant species including 50 aquatic plants. Though, the park is home to a varied wildlife, the presence of a significant number of famous Royal Bengal tigers makes it one of the most sought after wildlife destinations in India. You can spot a tiger while drinking on the banks of the lakes and watering holes in the evening.

Besides tigers, here you can spot a significant number of other wild animals including panthers, chital, sambar, jackal, hyena, black buck, chinkara, wild boars, mongoose, Indian hare, porcupines, sloth bear, langur, civets, flying foxes, monitor lizards and the never ending list goes on. The park also has a large number of exotic and colourful birds. The scenic spots and sceneries of the park are ideal for taking the snapshots.

Other attractions in the Ranthambore National Park include the Ranthambore Fort-probably the oldest fort in Rajasthan- and the Jogi Mahal- a beautiful forest rest house- that has the second largest Banyan tree in India. Besides, you can visit many tourist attractions located in the proximity of the park.

KEOLADEO GHANA NATIONAL PARK

An ornithologists' delight, Keoladeo Ghana National Park, popularly known as Bharatpur Bird Sanctuary was declared a National Park in 1983. This 29 sq km park is one of the world's greatest heronries. Its shallow, fresh water marsh attracts thousands of migratory birds. Over 10,000 nests of egrets, darters, cormorants, grey herons and storks hatch nearly 20,000 to 30,000 chicks every year. There is an infinite variety of migratory birds. Mammals like the sambhar, blackbuck, chital, nilgai, fishing cat, otter and mongoose also roam freely here. Best time to travel to Bharatpur is August to February.

An ornithologists' delight, Keoladeo Ghana National Park in Rajasthan, popularly known as Bharatpur Bird Sanctuary is sandwiched between historical cities of Agra and Jaipur. This 29 sq km park, approximately 10 sq km of which comprises of marshes and bogs, is one of the world's greatest heronries and historical in its own way.

The Maharaja of Bharatpur is credited for creating the national park in 1890, though conservation was the last thing on his mind. The government banned the indiscriminate shooting of birds in 1965. Conservation efforts originally started by Dr. Salim Ali received a further impetus when the area was deemed a National Park in March 1982. In 1985, Keoladeo Ghana in Bharatpur was accepted as a World Heritage Site.

Keoladeo Ghana or Bharatpur Bird Sanctuary hosts a variety of bird species from across the globe. Close to 380 species of birds are found. Its shallow, fresh water marsh attracts thousands of migratory birds. Over 10,000 nests of egrets, darters, cormorants, grey herons and storks hatch nearly 20,000 to 30,000 chicks every year. There is an infinite variety of migratory birds, making it one of the most inviting destinations in the world for ornithologists, amateurs and nature lovers. Mammals like the sambhar, blackbuck, chital, nilgai, fishing cat, otter and mongoose also roam freely here.

The bird most popular among tourists and ornithologists is the Siberian crane. According to field experts, this bird is known to travel distances of up to 6,500 km migrating from the Ob River basin region (Aral mountains, Siberia). Conservationists are working hard to protect the Siberian crane species as they are on the verge of extinction.

Apart from Feredunkenar in Iran, Keoladeo Ghana Sanctuary is the only place where the Siberian crane migrates. The cranes arrive in December and stay until early March. According to ornithologists, unlike its Indian counterpart the Siberian crane feeds on Cypress Rotents grass (an underground aquatic root). The intriguing fact is that Siberian cranes have a mixed diet of vegetation, fish and other small creatures back home, but they adopt a vegetarian diet during their stay in India.

Other 'guests' at Keoladeo Ghana include huge birds like Dalmatian pelicans, which are two meters in length, and minute ones like the Siberian leaf warbler, which is merely the size of our index finger!

Several other species of cranes-corcomorants, egrets, darters, herons, storks, geese, ducks, eagles, hawks, shanks, stints, wagtails, wheatears, flycatchers, buntings, larks, spoonbills, kingfishers, owls and pipits-also make Keoladeo Ghana their temporary abode.

Bharatpur heronry is one of its kind and bustles with zealous activity. The production of chicks during the breeding season is put at about 30,000. This avian kingdom also hosts mammalian species like nilgai, sambhar, chital, black bucks, jungle cat and the wild boar. The large rock python (which is spotted at Python Point beyond Keoladeo temple) as well as its nemesis, the mongoose, are found in appreciable numbers.

The mode of transport for getting around the sanctuary is a bicycle. Cycle-rickshaws may also be hired. Boats are available for hire from the ticket checkpoint. Boating is an excellent idea for getting around the Keoladeo Lake and observing the birds at close quarters while on holidays in Keoladeo Ghana National Park or Bharatpur Bird Sanctuary in Rajasthan..

SARISKA NATIONAL PARK

Sariska Wildlife Sanctuary, located at about 34 km from Alwar town in Rajasthan, is one of the most famous tiger reserves of India. Spread over an area of 800 sq km, the sanctuary is well nestled in the Aravali hills, which support the growth of scrub-thorn arid forests, dry deciduous forests, and grasses, making it a haven for wild animals. The sanctuary is covered under the famous Project Tiger of India as it houses a significant number of tigers. The Sariska was declared a sanctuary in 1955 and attained the status of a National Park in 1979.

Though, the sanctuary is famous for tigers, it is home to a varied wildlife. Other wildlife in the park include leopards, sambar, jungle cat, jackal, hyena, flying fox, chinkara, chital, chausingha, wild boar, nilgai, civet, four-horned antelope, gaur, mongoose and porcupine among many others. The Park is also home to a variety of exotic and colourful birds, which includes peafowl, gray partridges, quails, sand grouses, white-breasted kingfishers, golden-backed woodpeckers, crested serpent eagles, vultures and horned owls and the never ending list goes on.

Besides, being a home to rich and varied flora and fauna, the park also houses some of the historical monuments and temples. You can visit the ruins of some of the temples of the 9th and the 10th centuries here, famous among them is the temple dedicated to Lord Shiva, a Hindu God. A magnificent 17th century castle located on a hilltop at Kanakwari is an added attraction for the tourists. The castle provides a panoramic view of Sariska's inhabitants specially birds. You can also visit, the Sariska Palace, now a heritage hotel, which has a history of its own.

BHENSROD GARH SANCTUARY

A fairly new sanctuary, it was established in 1983 and covers a total area of 229 sq km of scrub and dry deciduous forest. Leopards, chinkara, sloth bear can be spotted here if one is lucky. The best time to plan you safari in Bhensrod Garh Sanctuary is between October and May.

DARRAH SANCTUARY

Previously the hunting ground of the Kota Maharajas, this sanctuary was established in 1955 and covers an area of 266 sq km. This hilly sanctuary with its thick forests is worth a visit during your travel to Rajasthan. The animals here include wolf, sloth bear, chinkara and leopard. The best time for Darrah Sanctuary safari is between February and May.

DESERT NATIONAL SANCTUARY

Established in 1980, it is a colossal park sprawling on 3162 sq km. It has shrubs and trees in addition to rolling sand dunes. The wildlife wealth here comprises fox, desert cat, hare, spiney tail uromastix and sand fish. Thousands of sparrows, imperial sand grouse, bustards, falcons and eagles migrate here during the winter. Best time to visit is September to March.

JAISAMAND SANCTUARY

Established in 1957, this sanctuary is located beside the man-made lake of the same name. Covering a total area of 160 sq km, it harbours sloth bear, leopard, chital, chinkara, wild boar and a number of birds. Some crocodiles and fish can also be spotted here. Best time to visit is between November and January.

KUMBHALGARH SANCTUARY

The majestic Kumbhalgarh Fort overlooks the 578 sq km sanctuary. The Aravalis hills, which remain barren for most of the year, turn green rains and provide shelter to sloth bear, leopard, flying squirrel. It is also the only sanctuary where the

Indian wolf is breeding successfully. Best time for tours here is March to May and September to November.

MOUNT ABU SANCTUARY

The highest point of Aravalis, the Guru Shikhar, lies in this 289 sq km sanctuary. Established in 1960, this provides shelter to the common langaur, wild boar, sambhar and leopard. The grey jungle fowl can also be spotted here. Besides a number of flowering trees enhance the beauty of this place.

Other wildlife sanctuaries in Rajasthan include Sitamata, Darrah, Chambal, Tal Chapper, Jamwa Ramgarh, Kaila Devi, Van Vihar, Ramgarh, Shergarh, Todgarh-Rad and Jawahar Sagar.

RAJASTHAN WILDLIFE SANCTURAY

Ranthambore Wildlife Sanctuary: Ranthambhore, in the state of Rajasthan, is one of the smallest Project Tiger reserves. It's name comes from the vast fort that stands in the middle of the forest. The name Ranthambore is derived from two hills in the area, Ran and Thanbhor. Another version says that Ranthambhore was once called Rana Stambhapura or City of the Pillars of War!

The Ranthambhore National Park at the junction of the Aravalis and the Vindhayas is a unique juxtaposition of the natural and historical richness, standing out conspicuously in the vast, arid and denuded tract of eastern Rajasthan, barely 14 kms. from Sawai Madhopur.

The elegant Ranthambhore fort called the Jogi Mahal is now the forest rest house.

It spreads over a highly undulating topography varying from the gentle to the steep slopes; from flat topped hills of the Vindhayas to the conical hillocks and the sharp ridges of the Aravalis. An important geological feature the 'Great Boundary Fault' where the Vindhaya plateaus meet the Aravali hill ranges, meanders through the reserve. The National Park is bounded by the rivers

Chambal in the South and the Banas in the North. Pure stands of the Dhok interspersed with open grasslands of the plateaus, six large lakes - Gilai Sagar, Mansarovar, Malik talao, Raj Bagh and Padam Talao with in the National Park.

CLIMATE OF RAJASTHAN

The Climate of Rajasthan in northwestern India is generally arid or semi-arid and features fairly hot temperatures over the year with extreme temperatures in both summer and winter.

History

Under the Köppen climate classification the greater part of Rajasthan falls under Hot Desert(BWh) and remaining portions of the state falls under Hot Semi Arid(BSh); the climate of the state ranges from arid to semi-arid. Rajasthan receives low and variable-rainfalls and thereby is prone to droughts.

Seasons

Summer

Due to the Desert Geography, Temperatures frequently climb above 40 to 45 degrees Celsius in most places.

Due to its location Rajasthan has summers as the longest season.

In this time tourist activities are very low. The army reduces its patrol time.

Winter

The cold weather commences early in October and comes to an end in the middle of January.The climate in the cold weather is pleasant to very cold.

Monsoon

The state has two distinct periods of rainfall: rainfall due to the South-West Monsoon after summer and rainfall due to Western Disturbances.

Disasters

Drought and famine

Rajasthan receives low and variable rainfalls and thereby is prone to droughts.Availability of water is less due to absence of rivers and lakes.

Floods

Occasional floods in cities due to improper drainage occurs. Sometimes floods also occur in western Rajasthan due to impervious base rocks.

Pollution

In some industrial and urban centers pollution has been reported occasionally.

FLORA AND FAUNA OF RAJASTHAN

Rajasthan has been blessed with varied flora and fauna even when majority of its area is desert. The forest cover is also quite limited, despite these adversities, some unique flora and fauna can be witnessed. Northern Desert Thorn Forest type natural vegetation is found in this state. This vegetation is found in form of small clumps which are scattered in the state in open forms. As rainfall increases when we move from west to east, the size and density of these patches increases.

Desert ecosystem is prominently seen in Rajasthan and one of the best examples to witness the same is the Desert National Park located in Jaisalmer. This park is sprawled in an area of 3162 square km. One can see diverse fauna in this ecosystem. The desert's geological history can be traced back to its origin through the massive tree trunks and sea shells that have been fossilized here. Many resident as well as migratory birds have made this region their home. Kestrel, falcons, eagles, vultures, harriers and buzzards can be commonly seen. Tawny Eagles (Scientific Name- Aquila rapax), Short toed Eagles (Scientific Names- Circaetus gallicus), Laggar Falcons (Scientific Name-

Falco jugger), Spotted Eagles (Scientific Name-Aquila clanga) and kestrels are some of the most commonly seen birds in this region.

Another worth visiting place is the Ranthambore National Park. It is located in Sawai Madhopur and is considered to be a prominent Tiger Reserves in India. In 1973, this National Park became an integral part of Project Tiger.

Rare and unique herbs are found grown in Dhosi Hill area. It is situated in Jhunjhunu region. This place is also famous as Chyawan Rishi's Ashram" and this is where Chayawanprash was first formulated. This formulation is considered to be good for health. In Alwar district, another popular reserve is located, namely Sariska Tiger Reserve. About 107 km from Jaipur and 200 km away from Delhi, this reserve is famous among wild life lovers. This reserve is sprawled in about 800 square km area. In 1979, Tiger Reserve was declared as a National Park.

The great Indian bustard has been classed as critically endangeredsince 2011.

Located in Churu district, in Sujangarh another sanctuary is located. It is famous as Tal Chhapar Sanctuary. Nestled amidst Shekhawati region, this sanctuary houses a large populace of desert foxes and blackbuck. A popular predator, caracal, also referred to as the desert lynx can also be seen here. Prominent birds found in this region are sand grouse and partridge. Locally known as Godavan, the Great Indian Bustard is the state bird of Rajasthan. Since 2011, it has been declared as an endangered species.

Though a large percentage of the total area is desert with little forest cover, Rajasthan has a rich and varied flora and fauna. The natural vegetation is classed as Northern Desert Thorn Forest (Champion 1936). These occur in small clumps scattered in a more or less open form. The density and size of patches increase from west to east following the increase in rainfall.

The Desert National Park in Jaisalmer is spread over an area of 3,162 square kilometres (1,221 sq mi), is an excellent example of the ecosystem of the Thar Desert and its diverse fauna. Seashells and massive fossilised tree trunks in this park record the geological history of the desert. The region is a haven for migratory and resident birds of the desert. One can see many eagles, harriers, falcons, buzzards, kestrels and vultures. Short-toed snake eagles *(Circaetus gallicus)*, tawny eagles *(Aquila rapax)*, spotted eagles *(Aquila clanga)*, laggar falcons *(Falco jugger)* and kestrels are the commonest of these.

The Ranthambore National Park located in Sawai Madhopur, one of the well known tiger reserves in the country, became a part of Project Tiger in 1973.

The Dhosi Hill located in the district of Jhunjunu, known as 'Chayvan Rishi's Ashram', where 'Chyawanprash' was formulated for the first time, has unique and rare herbs growing.

The Sariska Tiger Reserve located in Alwar district, 200 kilometres (120 mi) from Delhi and 107 kilometres (66 mi) from Jaipur, covers an area of approximately 800 square kilometres (310 sq mi). The area was declared a national park in 1979.

Tal Chhapar Sanctuary is a very small sanctuary in Sujangarh, Churu District, 210 kilometres (130 mi) from Jaipur in the Shekhawati region. This sanctuary is home to a large population of blackbuck. Desert foxes and the caracal, an apex predator, also known as the *desert lynx*, can also be spotted, along with birds such as the partridge and sand grouse. The great

Indian bustard, known locally as the *godavan*, and which is a state bird, has been classed as critically endangered since 2011.

Wildlife protection

Reclining tiger, Ranthambore National Park

Rajasthan is also noted for its national parks and wildlife sanctuaries. There are four national park and wildlife sanctuaries: Keoladeo National Park of Bharatpur, Sariska Tiger Reserve of Alwar, Ranthambore National Park of Sawai Madhopur, and Desert National Park of Jaisalmer. A national level institute, Arid Forest Research Institute (AFRI) an autonomous institute of the ministry of forestry is situated in Jodhpur and continuously work on desert flora and their conservation.

Ranthambore National Park is 7 km from Sawai Madhopur Railway Station. it is known worldwide for its tiger population and is considered by both wilderness lovers and photographers as one of the best place in India to spot tigers. At one point, due to poaching and negligence, tigers became extinct at Sariska, but five tigers have been relocated there. Prominent among the wildlife sanctuaries are Mount Abu Sanctuary, Bhensrod Garh Sanctuary, Darrah Sanctuary, Jaisamand Sanctuary, Kumbhalgarh Wildlife Sanctuary, Jawahar Sagar sanctuary, and Sita Mata Wildlife Sanctuary.

Communication

Major ISP and Telecom companies are present in Rajasthan including Airtel, Data Infosys Limited, Reliance Limited, Jio, RAILTEL, Software Technology Parks of India (STPI), Tata Telecom and Vodafone. Data Infosys was the first Internet Service Provider(ISP) to bring internet in Rajasthan in April 1999 and OASIS was first private mobile telephone company.

Flora

On the eastern side of Aravali range, a sparse forest cover can be seen. It is just nine percent of the total state area. Thus, limited vegetation can be witnessed in the desert area. Here, trees with stunted growth, some grasses and thorny shrubs can be seen. Besides Northern Desert Thorn Forest type natural vegetation, another vegetation type seen here is ephemeral. It is seen only during monsoon season.

The most prolific vegetation seen in this state is Kejri or prosopis cineraria. This is found majorly in arid zone. Its shape is bean like and is known as sangria. It is not only used as fodder but also consumed as vegetable. It is considered as a delicacy in Rajasthan. Another popular desert vegetable is ker. Variety of shrubs and akaro (scientific name- calotropis precera) are also found in abundance. Since this is desert vegetation, the shrubs have a lot of thorns. Other plants growing here are thor (Scientific name- euphorbia caduca), babul (Scientific name- acacia nilotica), bordi (Scientific name-sizypus nummularia) and anwal (Scientific name- cassia aureculata). Some perennial grass species seen here is dhaman (Scientific name- cenhrus cikaris), sewan (Scientific name- lasiurus sindicus), bharut (Scientific name- cenchrus catharficus) and boor (Scientific name- cenchrus jwarancusa). These species not only help in binding the soil together but are also good fodder for cattle.

Creeper, shrubs, herbs and bushes dot the shallow wetland landscape in Eastern Rajasthan. Khejri (Scientific name- prosopis cineria) and babul (Scientific name- acacia nilotica) are seen in Keoladeo National Park. More than seventy species of trees can be seen in the Ranthambore National Park. Some prominent species are peepal (Scientific Name- ficus religlora), Dhak (Scientific Name- butea monosperma), ber (Scientific Name- zizyphus mauritiana), banyan (Scientific Name- ficus bengha lensis) and khajur (Scientific Name- phoenix sylvestris). 13 shrub varieties, 30 grass species and more than 100 medicinal species can be seen here. In Mount Abu which is a hill area, species like bamboo (Scientific name- dendor calamus strictus), salar (Scientific name- bowellia seriata), dhav (Scientific name- anogeisrus pendula) and jamun (Scientific name- syzygium cumini) are found. Rare species of wild roses, ferns and orchids can also be seen here.

In neighboring areas of Jaipur, dhav can be found in abundance. Other plant species see here are thor, solar, guggal, godal, shatawari, brahmi and adusa.

Fauna

A vivid spectrum of faunal wealth can be witnessed in Rajasthan. Here, one can see variety of reptiles, mammals and bird life. In various areas of this state, gazellas and antelopes are found. Jodhpur region is widely inhabited by Black Bucks (Scientific name- Kala hiran) and in sandy deserts, one can find Indian Gazelle (Scientific name- chinkara). In open plains, one can easily spot blue bull or nilgai. They can also be seen close to Aravalli range.In hilly regions, four-horned antelope (Scientific name- chau singha) can be spotted. Forests where open meadows in patches can be seen, spotted deer and sambar can be seen roaming around. In monkey family, langur and rhesus macaque (Common name- Bandar) can be seen close to Aravalli Range. Indian Tiger is the best representative of cat family in this state. Tigers that are now declared endangered species can be witnessed in National Parks of Sariska and Ranthambhore. Panther or leopard is another species that is threatened. They are found close to Aravallis rocky outcrops and open countryside located in Jodhpur region. Caracal and Jungle Cat can also be seen. In dog family, wolf, jackal and desert fox can be seen.

In erstwhile times, Maharajas used to hunt wild boar as this was one of their leisure activities. Wild boar can be seen close to Mount Abu.

In Ranthambhore's deciduous forests, Sloth bear can also be spotted. Small sized mongoose and common mongoose can also be seen in arid regions. These creatures live on birds, rodents and snakes. In reptile family, Indian chameleon, Indian python and garden lizard can be seen.

Ghariyal and crocodile can be seen in abundance in the lakes and rivers of this state. Many migratory birds also visit Rajasthan. The prominent among these is Siberian Crane that travels more than 6000 km to reach Bharatpur. In Keoladeo National Park, more than 375 bird species can be spotted. The black-necked stork which is tallest bird in the world can also be seen here. Black in colour, it is about 1.8 metres tall. At Sambar and Khichan, demoiselle cranes can also be seen. Grey patridge and Indian Bustard are rare species that can be seen in forests of Rajasthan,

Wildlife Attraction

A wide array of Wildlife Sanctuaries and National Parks also dot state landscape. The main wildlife sanctuaries and national parks in Rajasthan are Sariska Tiger Reserve located in Alwar, Keoladeo National Park located in Bharatpur, Desert National Park situated in Jaisalmer and Ranthambore National Park located in Sawai Madhopur. For tiger population, Sariska Wildlife Sanctuary and Ranhambhore National Park are famous all over the world. Avid photographers and wildlife enthusiasts love to visit these reserved areas to spot this huge beast in its true splendor. Major wildlife sanctuaries in Rajasthan are Darrah Sanctuary, Mount Abu Sanctuary, Kumbhalgarh Wildlife Sanctuary, Bhensrod Garh Sanctuary, Jaisamand Sanctuary, Sita Mata Wildlife Sanctuary and Jawahar Sagar Sanctuary.

Aerial Population

In Rajasthan, more than 450 bird species have been identified.

These species include birds that found their habitat in wetlands, forests, desert and grasslands. Hornbills, orioles, swallows, kingfishers, parakeets, mynas, warblers, robins, doves, flycatchers, barbets, quails, peacocks, drongos and woodpeckers are housed in Aravalli range. One of the most significant bird sanctuaries in India is Keoladeo Bird Sanctuary. Wetlands are also found in Eastern Rajasthan. The prominent migratory birds seen in this state are herons, spoonbills, open bills, storks, egrets and ibis. They visit this stay during winters. Common marbled, pintail, Baikal teal, gadwell, coot, shoveler, bar-headed geese, wigeon and graylag geese are included in waterfowl's category. The guests coming in winters are Siberian cranes while saras lives permanently in this park. Besides saras, egrets, moorhens, cormorants and storks can be spotted.

6

Economy

ECONOMY OF RAJASTHAN

Bajra field

Rajasthan is a mineral-rich state and has a diversified economy having agriculture, mining and tourism as its main engines of growth. The state mines produce gold, silver, sandstone, limestone, marble, rock phosphate, copper and lignite. It is the second largest producer of cement and contributes one tenth of the salt produced in India.

Rajasthan's economy is primarily agricultural and pastoral. Wheat and barley are cultivated over large areas, as are pulses, sugarcane, and oilseeds. Cotton and tobacco are the state's cash crops. Rajasthan is among the largest producers of edible oils in India and the second largest producer of oilseeds. Rajasthan is also the biggest wool-producing state in India and the main opium producer and consumer. There are mainly two crop seasons. The water for irrigation comes from wells and tanks. The Indira Gandhi Canal irrigates northwestern Rajasthan.

The Indira Gandhi Canal passes through the Thar Desert near Ramgarh, Jaisalmer

The main industries are mineral based, agriculture based, and textile based. Rajasthan is the second largest producer of polyester fibre in India. Several prominent chemical and engineering companies are located in the city of Kota, in southern Rajasthan. Rajasthan is pre-eminent in quarrying and mining in India. The Taj Mahal was built from the white marble which was mined from a town called Makrana. The state is the second largest source of cement in India. It has rich salt deposits at Sambhar, copper mines at Khetri, Jhunjhunu, and zinc mines at Dariba, Zawar mines and Rampura Agucha (opencast) near Bhilwara. Dimensional stone mining is also undertaken in Rajasthan. Jodhpur sandstone is mostly used in monuments, important buildings and residential buildings. This stone is termed as "chittar patthar". Jodhpur leads in Handicraft and Guar Gum industry. Rajasthan is also a part of the Mumbai-Delhi Industrial corridor is set to benefit economically. The State gets 39% of the DMIC, with major districts of Jaipur, Alwar, Kota and Bhilwara benefiting.

Crude oil and Mineral stones

Rajasthan is earning Rs. 150 million (approx. US$2.5 million) per day as revenue from the crude oil sector. This earning is expected to reach 250 million per day in 2013 (which is an increase of 100 million or more than 66 percent). The government of India has given permission to extract 300,000 barrels of crude per day from Barmer region which is now 175,000 barrels per day. Once this limit is achieved Rajasthan will become a leader in Crude extraction in Country. Bombay High leads with a production of 250,000 barrels crude per day. Once the limit of 300,000 barrels per day is reached, the overall production of the country will increase by 15 percent. Cairn India is doing the work of exploration and extraction of crude oil in Rajasthan.

Rajasthan also has reserves of low-silica limestone.

Agricultural production

Rajasthan is the largest producer of barley, mustard, pearl millet, coriander, fenugreek and guar in India.BhamaShah Mandi in Kota district is the Asia's largest mandi or market of coriander. Rajasthan produces over 72% of guar of the world and 60% of India's barley. Rajasthan is major producer of aloe vera, amla, oranges leading producer of maize, groundnut. Rajasthan is 2nd in production of cumin, gram and 3rd in seed spices. Rajasthan government had initiated olive cultivation with technical support from Israel.The current production of olives in the state is around 100–110 tonnes annually. Rajasthan is India's second largest producer of milk. Rajasthan has 13800 dairy co-operative societies.

TRANSPORT

Jaipur International Airport

Road Tunnel in Jaipur Rajasthan

NH 8 between Udaipur and Ahmedabad

Rajasthan is connected by many national highways. Most renowned being NH 8, which is India's first 4–8 lane highway. Rajasthan also has an inter-city surface transport system both in terms of railways and bus network. All chief cities are connected by air, rail and road.

Air

There are three main airports at Rajasthan – Jaipur International Airport, Jodhpur Airport, Udaipur Airport and the recently started Bikaner Airportand Jaisalmer. These airports connect Rajasthan with the major cities of India such as Delhi and Mumbai. There is another airport in Kota but is not open for commercial/civilian flights yet. One more airport at Kishangarh, Ajmer .i.e. Kishangarh Airport has been constructed by the Airport Authority of India.

Rail

Rajasthan is connected with the main cities of India by rail. Jaipur, Kota, Ajmer, Jodhpur, Bharatpur, Bikaner, Alwar, Abu Road and Udaipur are the principal railway stations in Rajasthan. Kota City is the only Electrified Section served by three Rajdhani Expresses and trains to all major cities of India. There is also an international railway, the Thar Express from Jodhpur (India) to Karachi (Pakistan). However, this is not open to foreign nationals.

Road

Rajasthan is well connected to the main cities of the country including Delhi, Ahmedabad and Indore by State and National Highways and served by Rajasthan State Road Transport Corporation (RSRTC) and Private operators. Now in March 2017,75 per cent of all national highways being built in Rajasthan according to the public works minister of Rajasthan.

AGRICULTURE

Wheat and barley are cultivated in large areas, as are pulses, sugarcane, and oilseeds. Cotton and tobacco are cash crops. Rajasthan is among the largest producers of edible oils in India and the second largest producer of oilseeds. Rajasthan is also the biggest wool-producing state in India. There are mainly two crop seasons Kharifand Rabi. The main source of irrigation is wells and tanks. The Indira Gandhi Canal irrigates northwestern Rajasthan.

Rajasthan is largest producer of rapeseed, bajra, mustard and wool in India and second largest producer of oilseeds and spices and milk. Rajasthan is third largest producer of soya bean and coarse cereals in India.

Rajasthan is also the leading producer of milk in North India. Saras milk product brand of Rajasthan Co-operative Milk Producer Union has its outlets in Jaipur and New Delhi.

Industries

Rajasthan is a leading investment destination in India after Maharashtra and Gujarat because of its environment, law and order situation, infrastructure, investment climate and favourable population density. Areas facing NCR such as Bhiwadi are now popular with automobile and manufacturing companies. Many of the small scale suppliers and vendors have opted to shift inside Rajasthan border from Gurgaon in Haryana because of power shortage and infrastructure issues there.

Rajasthan State Industrial Development and Investment Corporation (RIICO) provides facilities for development. Rajasthan is now the preferred destination for IT companies, and North India's largest integrated IT park is located in Jaipur and is named as Mahindra World City Jaipur covering nearly 3,000 acres (12 km) of land. Some of the companies operating in Rajasthan include Infosys, Genpact, Wipro,Truworth, Deusche Bank, NEI, MICO, Honda Siel Cars, Coca-Cola, Gillete etc.

Mining

Rajasthan is pre-eminent in quarrying and mining in India. Hindustan Zinc, headquartered in Udaipur, Rajasthan is India's only and world's leading integrated Zinc, Lead and Silver producer. With its large scale operations of smelting and mining in various districts of Rajasthan, the company has contributed to the socio-economic development of the state. The state is the largest source of cement. Rajasthan is largest cement producing state of India. It has rich salt deposits at Sambhar, coppermines at Khetri and zinc mines at Dariba and Zawar. This is a chart of output of major minerals of Rajasthan.

Mineral	National Share
Wollastonite	100%
Jasper	100%
Zinc concentrate	99%
Fluorite	96%
Gypsum	93%
Marble	90%
Asbestos	89%
Soapstone	87%
Lead concentrate	80%
Phosphate rock	75%
Ball clay	71%
Calcite	70%
Sandstone	70%
Flaggy limestone	70%
Feldspar	70%

Tourism

Tourism is flourishing in Rajasthan. The palaces of Jaipur, lakes of Udaipur, and desert forts of Jodhpur, Bikaner & Jaisalmer are among the most common destinations for tourists. Tourism accounts for fifteen percent of the state's domestic product. Many old and neglected palaces and forts have been converted into heritage hotels. Tourism has increased employment in the hospitality sector.

Handicrafts

A spin-off of tourism has been the growth of the handicrafts industry.

INDUSTRY

The enterprise of the Rajasthani's is evident in the large number of small scale industrial units which have sprung up all over the state. There are large deposits of zinc and copper and these are being exploited for the development of industries dependant on these metals. It has large deposits of gypsum and lignite and mica. It has a large production of cotton and the textile industries has been coming up in several places in Rajasthan. Among the other private sector industries are cement, ball bearings, sugar, caustic soda and other chemicals.

INDUSTRIAL POLICY

Preamble

1. Rajasthan has been in the forefront of Economic Reforms. It was the first State in the country to adopt the International Competitive bidding route for setting up power projects. It was also the first in the country to announce a State Road Policy, facilitating the entry of private enterprise in the Roads sector. A new, simplified Sales Tax Act has been introduced by the State Government. The Mineral, Marble and Granite policies of 1994 have promoted scientific exploration and exploitation of the State's rich minerals. The Industrial Policy 1994 has brought about a significant change in its investment climate. The Rural Non Farm Policy of 1995- the first of its kind in the country - has helped focus efforts on growth and employment through rural industrialisation.
2. With a series of policy initiatives taken in the last few years, most roadblocks to the private sector's entry in Infrastructure have been removed. The State is poised

for significant developments in the Power Sector. The prospects for development of Solar energy are promising. There are indications of a significant oil and natural gas reserve, which could change the face of Western Rajasthan's economy.

3. Rajasthan is now among the six fastest growing States of the country. Its Eighth Plan Outlay constituted an increase of 283% over that of the Seventh Plan. During the past five years the average growth rate of investment in the large and medium sector has been 33% and in the SSI sector over 15%. Over the same period, exports from the State have grown at an annual average rate of 53%.
4. The experience of implementing the State's 1994 Industrial Policy has also brought to light certain deficiencies and practical problems, which need to be redressed. There are areas like Infrastructure and Human Resource Development which require even greater attention than has been accorded in the past. The New Industrial Policy of the State is thus an exercise to reflect these developments and to launch new initiatives to take advantage of the emerging opportunities.

Objectives : The principal objective of the new Policy is to make Rajasthan the most preferred State for investment in the identified sectors and to ultimately achieve global competitiveness. While governed by this basic goal, the Policy will lay special emphasis on accelerating the overall pace of Industrial growth, increasin employment opportunities, improving productivity, ensuring sustainable development and strengthening the SSI, Tiny and Cottage Industry sector.

Strategy

1. The above objectives will be achieved by adopting a strategy which enables focused growth. Thus, the new strategy envisages development of clusters offering economies of agglomeration and thrust sectors.
2. The task of improving infrastructure would be given the highest priority. The plans for infrastructure development

will take into account the resource endowment and the growth potential of each area.

3. Special emphasis will be given to the development of Thrust sectors, which have been identified keeping in view their infrastructural requirements, growth potential and the capacity to generate employment.
4. Simplification of rules and procedures, timely and smooth delivery of services will receive continued attention. Special efforts will be made for developing Government - Industry partnership in the implementation of the Policy.
5. Greater emphasis will be laid on development of human resources for emerging requirements of industry.
6. The basic approach of all the initiatives will be to encourage increasingly greater participation of private enterprise in the State's economic growth.

Infrastructure

- The overall approach towards the development and upgradation of infrastructure will be a combination of optimum utilization of the State's resources and involvement of the private sector. Specific measures will be taken to develop. Sectoral Clusters taking into account the needs of the targeted industry.
- *Board of Infrastructure Development and Investment*: The Board of Investment has been reconstituted as the Board of Infrastructure Development and Investment to ensure greater focus on industry-related infrastructure. It will ensure formulation of perspective plans for different regions, inter-sectoral coordination and effective monitoring for timely provision of facilities in industrial areas.
- *Project Development Corporation:* Based on the Memorandum of Understanding signed with Infrastructure Leasing and Financial Services Limited (IL&FS) and Housing Development and Finance Corporation (HDFC) a Project Development Corporation

(PDCOR) has been set up in the private sector, with equity participation by the State Government. The company will offer Investment Banking Reports on commercially profitable projects, tie up finances and offer projects for implementation to prospective investors.

- *Establishment of Business Centres:* In important industrial areas of the State, establishment of Business Centres in the private sector will be encouraged. Rajasthan State Industrial Development and Investment Corporation Ltd. (RIICO) will provide land and/or buildings for these Centres where facilities like office and conference space, telephone, fax and photo copying facilities etc. would be available to entrepreneurs.
- *Special Industrial Complexes:* Special Industrial Complexes are being developed in the State by RIICO to meet the requirements of specific industries, particularly of thrust sectors, at the following locations:

1. Gems & Jewellery EPIP & Gem Park, Jaipur
2. Hosiery Chopanki, Bhiwadi
3. Auto Ancilliary Ghatal (Bhiwadi) & Sitapura (Jaipur),
4. Ceramics Khara, (Bikaner)
5. Software Technology EPIP, (Jaipur)
6. Electronics & Telecomm. Kukas, (Jaipur)
7. Textiles Bhilwara, Sanganer, Sitapura, Pali, Jodhpur, Balotra
8. Agro Industries IGNP Area
9. Leather Manpur-Macheri
10. Wool Industries Beawar, Bikaner
11. Handicrafts Shilpgram, (Jodhpur and Jaisalmer)
12. Dimensional Stone Kishangarh, Udaipur, Chittorgarh

Other Related Aspects

1. Efforts will be made to reduce project implementation time through provision of essential infrastructure facilities like roads, power, street lights and water supply. An

industrial area will be declared as developed after these specific facilities have been provided. Service charges will be recovered only with effect from the date of declaration of the industrial area as developed. Missing links in the existing industrial areas would be identified and steps taken to provide the required facilities.

2. Efforts would be made to provide social infrastructure facilities like housing, schools, hospitals/dispensaries, shopping centres etc. in important industrial areas. Some of the industrial areas would be developed as industrial townships.
3. The Industrial Complexes being developed in the National Capital Region of the State would be further strengthened in terms of infrastructure facilities.
4. The entire belt around N.H.8 from Jaipur to Bhiwadi would be taken up for integrated industrial development. A blue print for development of industrial townships in this belt would be prepared keeping in view the increased flow of investments in this region.

Development of Integrated Industrial Parks (IIPs) and Industrial Model Towns (IMTs)

1. Development of Integrated Industrial Parks (IIPs) as joint venture projects with RIICO, or in the private sector will be actively encouraged by undertaking the following measures:
   (a) Formulation of schemes for development of IIPs in the private sector on BOT (Build-Operate-Transfer) or BOOM (Build-Own-Operate-Maintain) basis, while dovetailing them with the overall development plans of the region.
   (b) Encouraging promotion of IIPs through equity participation by RIICO and assistance from other agencies of the Government.
   (c) Devising a policy for allotment of land to private sector on the basis of a transparent mechanism.

(d) Concessions available to industrial units set up in RIICO's industrial areas would also be available to units located in the IIPs and Industrial Parks in the Private Sector

2. Development of industrial areas in the private sector was earlier prohibited within 10 Kms radius of RIICO's industrial areas; this distance has now been reduced to 5 Kms. Rajasthan Industrial Areas Allotment Rules, 1959 have been amended to facilitate the development of industrial areas/estates in the private sector.

Land Conversion: Despite efforts made in the past, entrepreneurs have been facing difficulties in securing conversion of land from agricultural to industrial. To resolve this problem, provision has been made for automatic conversion of land upto 5 hectares. On expiry of 30 days from the date of application for conversion to the appropriate Revenue authority the conversion shall be deemed to have taken place and the concerned Revenue Authority/GM, DIC will issue a certificate of deemed conversion. The concerned Tehsildar/Gram Panchayat shall make necessary entries in the land records within 7 days.

Maintenance of Industrial Areas

1. Proper upkeep and maintenance of the existing industrial areas will be ensured by RIICO. Wherever possible, Local Bodies, Industries Associations and other organisations will be associated with this activity and on their request areas can be handed over to them for this purpose.
2. Advisory Committees comprising, interalia, industry representatives, will be set up in respect of industrial areas to advise on:

   (a) Maintenance and improvement of the existing areas; and

   (b) Redressal of grievances.

The scope of work of these Advisory Committees has been indicated in Annex-I.

Settlement Committees : RIICO and RFC have constituted three tier Settlement Committees for resolving disputes pertaining to entrepreneurs. These Committees are fully empowered to decide matters falling within their jurisdiction. This would reduce future litigation and pending Court cases can also be settled by these Committees. The details of constitution and working of these Committees has been given in Annexure-II.

Power

1. Rajasthan has been recognised as one of the two leading states, which have vigorously pursued Power Sector Reforms. According to the assessment carried out by the Ministry of Power during the year 1996-97, the difference between the Peak Demand and Peak Demand met in Rajasthan was only 5.6% - the lowest among the twenty major States of the country. In addition, in terms of Plant Load Factor the State with a PLF of 75.6% was ranked the second in the country. Substantial private sector investment in power generation is being encouraged.
2. Two units of 250 MW each are expected to be commissioned at Suratgarh Stage-I Project during 1998 and 1999, respectively. In addition, the following major power plants are scheduled to be commissioned in the IX Five Year Plan and early years of X Five Year Plan:

S.No.	***Projects in Pipeline***	***Capacity***
1.	Dholpur Power Project based on Liquid Fuel.	700 MW
2.	Barsingsar Power Project based on Lignite.	500 MW
3.	Suratgarh Stage-II Power Project based on Coal.	500 MW
4.	Kapurdi & Jalipa Projects based on Lignite.	1200 MW
	TOTAL	2900 MW

3. Captive power plants will be freely permitted. No permission from RSEB would be required.
4. State Government has recently announced a Captive Power Plant Policy. The details of the policy shall be issued by the Energy Department shortly.

5. As far as possible RSEB shall make arrangements to ensure uninterrupted supply of power to continuous process industry, export oriented units and units set up in EPIP.
6. All industrial areas on rural feeders will be connected to urban/industrial feeders in a phased manner for better quality of power and the cost to be incurred thereon shall be borne by RSEB and RIICO equally.
7. As far as possible, land for power plants to be set up in private sector will be allotted by RIICO close to the grid station of RSEB, at rates applicable for industrial land on priority basis.
8. Provisional fuel surcharge will henceforth be revised on a quarterly basis to avoid an undue burden on industrial units at a later stage.
9. Reduction in contract demand to units supplying surplus power to RSEB will be freely permitted. Where the contract demand is reduced to zero, *i.e.*, the industrial consumer runs his plant entirely with his own power, no minimum charge shall be levied.
10. New large industrial consumers will be required to pay for the first six months on the basis of actual consumption and for the next six months, on the basis of actual consumption or 50% of the minimum charges, whichever is higher.
11. A system of deemed sanction has been started by RSEB for extension of power contract demand. Similarly, a system of deemed sanction for reduction in load has also been introduced.

Telecommunication

1. Special efforts will be made to provide efficient and reliable Telecommunication Facilities in Industrial areas.
2. In case of new industrial areas, RIICO will take recourse to Bulk booking in advance so that entrepreneurs are able to secure telephone connections without delay.

3. Cellular phones facility is already available in the following towns of the State:
    1. Jaipur
    2. Ajmer
    3. Udaipur
    4. Jodhpur
    5. Kota

This facility is proposed to be introduced in other industrially important locations like Alwar, Bhiwadi, Pali, Beawar etc.

Railways

1. Under the unigauge scheme of the Railways, the State has taken a major leap forward with the ongoing and proposed programmes of conversion of metre guage lines into broad guage. Most of the metre guage lines have already been converted and all the major cities of the state except Udaipur and Bhilwara have been linked with broad guage. Jaipur has been linked to major industrial cities like Mumbai, Calcutta, Chennai, Hyderabad, Delhi, Indore and many other towns.
2. Vigorous efforts will be made to ensure that Bhilwara and Udaipur are also connected with broad guage expeditiously.
3. The proposal to provide rail link to Bhiwadi on priority will be pursued with the Railways.

Road Network

1. The State Government has promulgated a Road Policy in 1995 to facilitate private sector participation in construction of toll roads, bridges and by passes. Private sector participation in Road sector is being actively encouraged. Under this policy three works of roads/ bridges have already been awarded to private sector on B.O.T. basis and several other works are being taken up.

2. The State's road network extends to 0.75 lacs kms. on 31st March 1997 comprising National Highways, State Highways, District Roads and other roads. Of the existing State Highway network, a length of 1500 kms. will be improved with World Bank assistance during the 9th Five Year Plan.
3. The National Highway No.8, from Delhi to Bombay via Jaipur-Ajmer-Udaipur-Ahmedabad is being converted into a four-lane highway. The stretch between Jaipur and Kotputli has already been completed and the remaining portion between Kotputli and Delhi is expected to be completed shortly. Jaipur-Ajmer section is being taken up in the second phase.
4. In order to improve access to important industrial areas, the State Government and RIICO will take up works for improvement of vital link roads to important industrial areas like Bhiwadi, Khushkhera, Matsya (Alwar), Hirawala, Bindayaka, Kaladera (Jaipur), Growth Centres at Dholpur, Brij (Bharatpur), Gudli (Udaipur) etc. The total length of these road links will be about 100 kms. Some of the important link roads have been shown in the map at Annex-III.

Port Access : With a view to ensuring expeditious despatch of export cargo, the State Government is exploring the feasibility of securing a direct access to Marine Port in Gujarat. A feasibility study for the purpose has been completed and a dialogue has been initiated with Governments of neighbouring states for joining hands to develop a berth facility at Kandla.

Air Transport

1. Important cities of the state like Jaipur, Udaipur and Jodhpur are well connected by Air. Facilities at Jaipur airport have been upgraded and it has now started receiving Chartered International flights.
2. Air Taxi Operators (ATO's), will be encouraged to expand their services in the state. The use of State Government's

existing air strips numbering 19 and some other facilities has already been offered to ATOs so as to facilitate their operations.

AGRICULTURE

There are mainly two crop seasons. The major crops sown during the months of June-July and harvested in Sep-Oct are bajra, Jowar, Pulses, maize and ground nut.

Main Rabi crops for which sowing operations start during Oct-Nov and harvested in March-April include wheat, barley, pulses, gram and oil seeds.

Among oil seeds, rape and mustard is the most important. Fruits and vegetables are also sown throughout the state where soil especially suits this type of cultivation. Fruit trees grown include orange, lemon, pomegranate, guava and mango. The main source of irrigation is wells and tanks.

DEVELOPMENT AND PLANNING

Power Policy: Rajasthan has been recognised as one of the two leading states that have vigorously pursued power sector reforms. The focus of these reforms is to provide an environment that is conducive for private sector participation. The key components of the power sector reforms are as follows: Management of demand to conserve and promote efficient use of energy and ensure environmental protection. Tariff reforms. First-level revision in tariffs has already been approved by the State Cabinet. Establishment of an independent regulatory commission to regulate the functioning of the power sector on sound commercial principles. Unbundling the State's electricity board into separate, Government-owned generation, transmission and distribution companies. Promotion of competition among various power sector entities. Corporatisation and commercialisation of the emerging power sector entities to make the power sector attractive for potential investors. The State Government will retain the role of policy formulation.

STATE WATER POLICY

The Need for a State Water Policy: Water is a prime natural resource, a basic human need and a precious asset of the State. Planning, development, operation and maintenance of all water resources to support the growth of the state economy and the well being of the population, in response to the growing need for drinking water, agricultural products, industrial production and electricity, a general improvement of living conditions and employment is of utmost importance. Planning and development of water resources need to be governed by the state's perspectives. The requirement of utilising all available water resources, surface and ground, in a judicious and equitable, as well as sound economic manner needs a well defined State Water Policy.

The State of Rajasthan is the second largest state in the country covering an area of 34.271 Million ha which is more than 10% of the total geographical area of the country. About 5% of the total population of the country resides in the state and it has more than 15.7 million ha of land suitable for agriculture. The State of Rajasthan is one of the driest states of the country and the total surface water resources in the state are only about 1% of the total surface water resources of the country. The rivers of the state are rainfed and identified by 14 major basins divided into 59 subbasins.

The surface water resources in the state are mainly confined to south and south-eastern parts of the State. There is a large area in western part of the state which does not have any defined drainage basin. Thus the water resources in the state are not only scarce but have highly uneven distribution both in time and space.

The ground water also plays an important role especially in agriculture and drinking water supply. The situation of ground water exploitation is also not satisfactory as in areas where surface irrigation is provided there is a tendency of not using ground water for agriculture which creates problem of water table rise and even water logging. On the contrary, in large areas of the State, ground water is being over exploited and the water table in some areas is going down even at the rate of 3 metre per year.

This background leads to the formulation of the following water resources development and management objectives:

a. Development of all utilisable water resources to the maximum possible extent, including surface water - local and imported - ground-water and waste water, for optimal economic development and social well-being.
b. Assuring an integrated and multi-disciplinary approach to planning, evaluation, approval and implementation of irrigation and drainage projects, including river basin management, of surface and ground water.
c. Optimisation of water resources exploitation and raising the level of reliability of supplies through conjunctive use of surface and ground water.
d. Judicious and economically sound allocation of water resources to different sectors, with drinking water supply as a first priority.
e. Optimum utilisation of water resources to maximise production in all user sectors.
f. Providing flood protection and drainage facilities, as well as assuring minimal supplies during drought periods.
g. Maintenance of water quality at acceptable standards and reduction of water resources' pollution by urban and industrial sewage.
h. Ensuring proper functioning of existing structures, conveyance systems and other assets through adequate maintenance and operation.
i. Minimising adverse impacts of water resources development on the natural environment and on population affected by project implementation works.
j. Promoting beneficiaries' participation in all aspects of water planning and management, with particular emphasis on Water User Associations intended to manage

and maintain irrigation systems, both physically and financially.

k. Motivating and encouraging water conservation through appropriate and socially acceptable water rates, introduction of water-saving devices and practices in all sectors, and educational campaigns.

l. Advancing the technological and scientific level of all the staff in the water sector through intensification of applied research, technology transfer, training and education.

m. Ensuring well coordinated and efficient decision making, planning, design, execution and operation and maintenance activities among all GOR agencies.

n. Facilitating private initiative in development, operation and management of water projects.

o. Emphasis to be given for recharge of ground water aquifers to mitigate the crisis of drinking water supply and demand of drinking water supply and for industrial and other purposes.

Information System: The prime requisite for resources planning is a well developed information system. There should be free exchange of data among the various agencies and duplication in data collection should be avoided. Timely availability of reliable information, conveniently accessible to all users, is necessary as a tool for integrated planning of new projects, and for following up the performance of existing systems and the status of water resources. Following actions shall be taken in this regard:

a. Setting up of a central information centre for the entire water sector of Rajasthan.

b. Clear definition of duties and responsibilities of those charged with data collection.

c. Detailing of main reports to be generated.

Maximizing Water Availability: Due to the high variability of hydro-meteorological phenomena not all the potentially available resources can be harnessed and made utilisable. The overwhelming interest of the State is to bring, by physical and managerial measures, as much of the potentially available resources into beneficial utilisation as is physically and economically feasible.

The resources shall be conserved and the availability for use augmented by measures for maximising retention and minimising losses. Following actions shall be taken for maximising water availability:

a. Comprehensive and integrated water resource planning shall be done for the State on the basis of hydrological units *i.e.* basin or a sub-basin.
b. Water resources potentials, both surface and ground, shall be assessed.
c. Basin-wise and State-level water resources development and environmental plans shall be prepared.
d. Water resources development projects shall be prioritised on economic, social and financial criteria to aid in budget allocation.
e. Waste water reclamation shall be considered in all basin plans.
f. Efficient water application and utilisation practices shall be encouraged.
g. A Central Planning Authority for policy related issues for integrated water resources development and management shall be created.
h. Traditional water harvesting practices shall be preserved and encouraged.
i. Projects for artificial recharge of ground water shall be prepared.
j. Inter basin transfer projects shall be prepared based on a State-wide perspective, after taking into account the requirements within the basins.
k. The case for full utilisation of State's share in Ganga waters shall be pursued.

Project Planning: Water resources development planning shall aim at assuring accelerated growth by contributing to the

State's economic and social advancement, and improving the general social and economic conditions of the population, while keeping the environmental and ecological balance. The State Water Policy shall be reflected in all plans recommended for implementation. Special attention shall be given to the non-structural elements of this policy, aimed at achieving the objectives of reduction of poverty, basic food self-sufficiency, overall economic growth, environmental well-being, progress of weaker sections of the population, etc.

Water resource development projects shall as far as possible be planned and developed as comprehensive and multi-purpose projects. All present and predictable future demands, including irrigation, domestic and livestock demand, industries, thermal and hydroelectric power stations, pisci-culture and recreation, and all sources of natural water as well as reclaimed waste-water must be considered. Provision for drinking water shall be a primary consideration. The study of the impact of a project, during its construction period as well as during its operational life, on human lives, settlements, occupations, economic and other social aspects, shall be an essential component of project planning.

Time and cost overruns and deficient realisation of benefits characterising most irrigation projects shall be overcome by upgrading the quality of project preparation and management. The under-funding of projects shall be obviated by an optimal allocation of resources, having regard to the early completion of ongoing projects as well as the need to reduce regional imbalances.

The following institutional and procedural reforms and manpower development in projects shall be carried out:

Institutional Reforms

a. integrated long and short term planning of water resources development.
b. economic analysis and feasibility studies of projects.
c. monitoring and evaluation of existing projects.

d. drafting annual and multi-annual expenditure programmes for the entire water sector and obtaining approval.
e. encourage private initiative in water sector.

Human Resources Development

a. Introduce training courses and professional career incentives, and foster professional dedication, with emphasis on client management.

Procedural Reforms

a. Improvement in process of project planning, sanctioning, bidding, etc.
b. Define accountability and authority.
c. Define information flow routes and access to data.
d. Establish guidelines for priority in public spending in water sector.

Maintenance and Modernisation: For maintaining the existing structures and systems in satisfactory condition and timely modernisation, the following actions shall be taken:

a. Adequate budget for maintenance, repair, modernisation of existing structures and systems shall be allocated.
b. Water rates shall be increased and collections shall be improved.
c. Orders and instructions for inspections / reporting of maintenance, repair and replacement works shall be issued.
d. Maintenance oriented training programmes shall be undertaken.
e. Water User Associations shall be encouraged to undertake maintenance, repairs and modernisation of works.

Safety of Structures: The Dam Safety Organisation shall be reinforced and supported, at State level, for ensuring the trained staff in improved inspection, analysis and evaluation techniques of dams and other structures. Guidelines issued by State authorities on the subject shall be kept under constant review and periodically updated and re-formulated Dam Safety Legislation may be enacted to ensure proper inspection, maintenance and surveillance of existing dams and also to ensure proper planning, investigation, design and construction for safety of new dams.

Ground-water Development: Exploitation of ground-water resources should be so regulated as not to exceed recharging possibilities, and also to ensure social equity. There should be a periodical reassessment on a scientific basis of ground-water potentials, taking into consideration the quality of the water available and economic viability. Following steps shall be taken in this regard:

Legal : Existing laws shall be amended /new legislation shall be enacted.

Organisational : Organisational structures and procedures shall be changed. Attempt to control deep drilling through licensing and control on private operators shall be made.

Social: Public awareness for self-control in ground water exploitation from WUAs shall be fostered.

Educational: Sense of water scarcity and need to conserve shall be developed.

Technological : Data collection shall be improved, conjunctive use of ground and surface water shall be planned, mathematical modelling of aquifer shall be done and artificial recharge of ground water shall be planned.

Environmental : The detrimental environmental consequences of over exploitation of ground water need to be effectively prevented.

Water Allocation Priorities

In the planning and operation of systems, water allocation priorities shall be to Drinking water, Irrigation, Power generation and Industrial and other uses in that order. However, these priorities might be modified if necessary in particular regions with reference to area specific considerations, and they may be different in the context of allocating water to existing consumers than in the context of planning the development of water resources for new consumers.

A detailed methodology for multi-priority analysis shall be developed for decision making in the Central Planning Authority to enable prioritisation in water resources planning and management. The demands of drinking water, irrigation, power generation, industrial and other uses shall be studied scientifically for appropriate development and allocation of funds.

Drinking Water

Adequate drinking water facilities shall be provided to the entire population both in urban and in rural areas. Future irrigation and multipurpose projects shall invariably include a drinking water component wherever there is no dependable alternative source of drinking water. Drinking water needs of human beings and animals shall be the first charge on any available water and following actions shall be taken to fulfil this need:

a. Increased budget shall be allocated for upgrading urban and rural domestic and livestock water supply.

b. Water rates shall be gradually increased to self-support the operation of urban and rural piped schemes.

c. Finance of rural water supply schemes shall be continued.

d. Water quality standards shall be ensured.

e. Strict control over activities which endanger sources such as hazardous wastes and sewage shall be exercised.

f. Privatisation in urban water supply especially for meter reading, billing etc. can be contracted out.

Irrigation Water

Irrigation planning, either in an individual project or in a basin as a whole, should take into account the irritability of land, cost-effective irrigation options possible from all available sources of water, and appropriate irrigation and drainage techniques. The irrigation intensity should be such as to extend the benefits of irrigation to as large as number of farm families as possible, keeping in view the need to maximise production.

Following measures shall be taken to ensure that the irrigation potential created is fully utilised, the gap between the potential created and its utilisation is removed, water allocation in an irrigation system is done with due regard to equity and social justice, disparities in the availability of water between head-reach and tail-end farms and between large and small farms should be obviated by adoption of a rotational water distribution system, supply of water on a volumetric basis subject to certain ceilings is introduced and there is close integration of water-use and land-use policies.

To achieve these objectives a multi-disciplinary and integrated approach will be followed under C.A.D. programme.

a. It shall be ensured that the Government regulations are adhered to by law and persuasion.

b. Farmers shall be encouraged to adopt high efficiency water equipments and practices and use of ground water in conjunction with surface water.

c. Water charges shall be reviewed and realistic water rates shall be introduced.

d. Reclamation of waterlogged/saline affected land by scientific methods should form a part of command area development programme.

Water Rates: Water rates shall be so decided that it conveys the scarcity value of water to users and foster the motivation for economy in water usage. Rates shall be gradually increased to cover the annual maintenance and operation charges and part of the fixed costs to assure undisturbed and timely supply of irrigation water. Water rates shall be rationalised with due regard to the interests of small and marginal farmers. It shall be accompanied by volumetric measurement of water consumption in all sectors.

Participation of Water Users: Farmers shall be involved in various aspects of management of irrigation systems, particularly in water distribution and collection of water charges through following measures:

a. Evaluating results of on-going pilot projects where farmers' participation has been introduced.
b. Introducing changes in legislation for fostering user participation in irrigation.
c. Giving priority of funds for rehabilitation and modernisation of irrigation projects to those projects where farmers are willing to organise into WUAs.
d. Assistance of voluntary agencies shall be taken in educating the farmers in efficient water use and water management.

Water Quality Monitoring: Both surface water and ground water as well as soil quality shall be regularly monitored for quality and a phased programme shall be undertaken for improvements in water quality.

Government shall issue orders to routinely enter future water and soil quality figures in the water resources database and publish ground-water statistics and maps for River Basins. Proposals for contracting the work of water sampling and analysis to private operators will be studied.

Effluents should be treated to acceptable levels and standards before discharging them in natural streams. Minimum flow should be ensured in the perennial streams for maintaining ecology and social considerations.

Water Zoning

Water Conservation and Efficiency of Utilization. The efficiency of utilisation in all the diverse uses of water should be improved and an awareness of water as a scarce resource should be fostered. Conservation consciousness shall be promoted through education, regulation, incentives and disincentives by taking following actions:

Domestic Sector

- Introduction of domestic water saving devices
- Water meters on all consumers.
- Progressive water tariff structure.
- Auditing of water balance from distribution systems. etc...

Industrial Sector

- Progressive water tariff.
- Water recycling facilities.
- Treated urban sewage water for cooling and other processes.

Agriculture Sector

- Water rates on volumetric basis should be kept sufficient for maintenance.
- Treated sewage water for non-edible crops.
- Saline water for tolerant crops.
- Improvement in irrigation practices and reduction of water losses.
- Pressure irrigation systems to be introduced

Watershed Management for each Basin

- Afforestation, soil conservation.
- Livestock management.
- Treatment and disposal of sewage.

Every drop of water needs to be conserved and optimally utilised for which detailed scheme shall be framed ensuring its time bound implementation.

Flood Control and Drainage Management: Sound watershed management through extensive soil conservation, catchment area treatment, preservation of forests and increasing the forest area and construction of check dams shall be promoted to reduce the intensity of floods. Adequate flood cushion shall be provided in water storage projects whenever feasible to facilitate better flood management. An extensive network for flood forecasting shall be established for timely warning to the settlements in the flood plains, along with the introduction of regulation for settlements and economic activity in the flood-prone zones to minimise loss of life and property caused by floods. Master plan for flood control and management for each flood prone basin / area shall be got prepared. Due consideration to provide proper drainage shall also be given to build up capabilities to tackle water logging and salinity problems.

Drought Management: Drought prone areas shall be made less vulnerable to drought associated problems through measures listed below. In planning water resource development projects, the needs of drought prone areas should be given priority. Relief works undertaken for providing employment to drought stricken populations should preferably be for drought proofing.

a. Continue efforts to assure water supply and livelihood to population and care for livestock.
b. Employment and direct provision of basic needs to population in times of crisis.
c. Drought-proofing of the area in measures such as plantation, dry farming.
d. Development of training and skills to enable population to supplement the earnings from agriculture.
e. Development of the ground water potential including recharging and the transfer of surface water from surplus areas wherever feasible and appropriate.

Training and Education: Standardised training shall be a part of water resources management and should cover all its aspects and all personnel involved in it, including farmers. The State shall also encourage education of the public at large.

Scholarships, study tours, incentives etc. shall be provided by the State to encourage and support training. Technology transfer shall be made obligatory on all technical assistance and consulting services. Emphasis on research on all matters related to water management shall also be given.

Legislation and Regulation: After a critical examination of rules, regulations, ordinances, legal and legislative measures related to the State's water sector has been made, with a view to improve and streamline their scope and cover in the legal framework all aspects pertaining to water resources management, protection of water quality, flood protection, drought proofing, abstraction licensing, water rights, etc. the Government shall introduce the following measures:

a. Enact the necessary amendments and additions to existing Act, rules, regulations, orders, decisions, etc.;
b. Ensure that the responsibilities and powers of Governmental agencies and the rights and obligations of individuals be clearly spelled-out in the relevant laws and regulations;
c. Ensure that the legislation would allow for easy implementation of policy decisions while protecting the interests of individuals and taking into account the administrative capacity to implement them;
d. Empower the appropriate agencies to carry out their obligations and responsibilities as implied by the public ownership of water projects, and spell out the administrative procedures necessary for coordinated, equitable and efficient control, as well as the resolution of conflicts which may arise from them;
e. Provide legal support for the formation of WUAs and handing over to them the distribution of water for irrigation and the maintenance of canals;
f. Establish rules and regulations for the involvement of the private sector in development and operation of water-related projects;
g. Provide in the law for an effective participation of farmers in the planning and decision making processes which involve users and public authorities;
h. Introduce the necessary legislation for a periodic amendment of water rates and tariff structures which would enable the full coverage of O&M expenditures, based,

as far as possible on volumetric metering of supplies, while motivating users to economise in the use of water, and catering for the weaker sections of the population;

i. Establish effective conflict resolution legal entities and procedures. The entire body of water-related laws and regulations will eventually be amalgamated into a State Water Law, which would, in addition to the above mentioned subjects, establish the State ownership of all the water resources within the State, as well as waters imported from outside the State under various agreements, and the requirement for any public or private entity or individual to obtain from the Government a permit to abstract surface water or ground-water, to utilise it, to sell or distribute it, or to dispose off after use. Permitting and enforcement rules and regulations will be spelled-out accordingly.

7

Tourism

TOURISM IN RAJASTHAN

Rajasthan is one of the most popular tourist destinations in India, for both domestic and international tourists. Rajasthanattracts tourists for its historical forts, palaces, art and culture with its slogan 'Padharo mahare desh'. Every third foreign tourist visiting India travels to Rajasthan as it is part of the Golden Triangle for tourists visiting India.

The palaces of Jaipur, lakes of Udaipur, and desert forts of Jodhpur, Bikaner & Jaisalmer are among the most preferred destinations of many tourists, Indian and foreign. Tourism accounts for eight percent of the state's domestic product. Many old and neglected palaces and forts have been converted into heritage hotels. Tourism has increased employment in the hospitality sector. The main sweet of this place is ghewar.

Rajasthan attracted 14 percent of total foreign visitors during 2009–2010 which is the fourth highest among Indian states. It is fourth also in Domestic tourist visitors. Tourism is a flourishing industry in Rajasthan. The palaces of Jaipur and Ajmer-Pushkar, the lakes of Udaipur, the desert forts of Jodhpur, Taragarh Fort(Star Fort) in Ajmer, and Bikaner and Jaisalmer rank among the most preferred destinations in India for many tourists both Indian and foreign. Tourism accounts for eight percent of the state's domestic product. Many old and neglected palaces and forts have been converted into heritage hotels. Tourism has increased employment in the hospitality sector.

Pushkar Lake, a sacred Hindu lake, is surrounded by fifty-two bathing ghats.

Rajasthan is famous for its forts, carved temples, and decorated havelis, which were built by Rajput kings in pre-Muslim era Rajasthan. Rajasthan's Jaipur Jantar Mantar, Mehrangarh Fort and Stepwell of Jodhpur, Dilwara Temples, Chittor Fort, Lake Palace, miniature paintings in Bundi, and numerous city palaces and haveli's are part of the architectural heritage of India. Jaipur, the Pink City, is noted for the ancient houses made of a type of sandstone dominated by a pink hue. In Jodhpur, maximum houses are painted blue. At Ajmer, there is white marble Bara-dari on the Anasagar lake. Jain Temples dot Rajasthan from north to south and east to west. Dilwara Temples of Mount Abu, Ranakpur Temple dedicated to Lord Adinath in Pali District, Jain temples in the fort complexes of Chittor, Jaisalmerand Kumbhalgarh, Lodurva Jain temples, Mirpur Jain

Temple of Sirohi, Sarun Mata Temple kotputli, Bhandasar and Karni Mata Temple of Bikaner and Mandore of Jodhpur are some of the best examples.

Palaces

Rajasthan is known for its historical hill forts & palaces, it is claimed as best place for tourism related to palaces. Following are some of major palaces in Rajasthan.

- Umaid Bhawan Palace: It is the largest Royal Palace in Rajasthan. It is also one of largest private residence in the world.
- Lake Palace: It is now a luxury hotel located in Pichola Lake, Udaipur.
- Hawa Mahal: It is known as "Palace of Wind" or "Palace of Breeze" because there are more than 950 Windows in the Palace.
- Rambagh Palace: Formerly a Royal Palace now converted into a Heritage Hotel.
- Devi Garh Palace: Formerly a palace now converted into a Heritage Hotel, In 2006, The New York Times named it as one if leading luxurious hotel in Indian subcontinent.

TOURISM AS INDUSTRY

Government of Rajasthan has granted status of the industry to tourism sector in the year 1989 and all the facilities and concession available to industries in the state would also be available to tourism units in the state as per rules in force.

Tourist Transport (Rail): Major destinations in Rajasthan are already on the rail Map. With conversion of Meter gauge to Broad gauge connectivity with major tourist entry points has been greatly augmented. Efforts will be made to arrange special tourist trains, with convenient timings to facilitate Tourist travel by rail. Special local site seeing by coach will be dovetailed by RTDC.

Broad gauge Palace-On-Wheels has already been launched in the year 1996-97 and it has proved to be extremely popular with International tourists and NRIs. Efforts would be made to launch an economy version of luxurious Palace-On-Wheels for budget tourists.

Road Transport: Due to inadequate air and rail links, surface transport assumes added importance in the context of Rajasthan. To upgrade essential road links external assistance would be sought to augment state plan resources.

Air-conditioned tourist coaches, tourist cars and specially designed non-air-conditioned sightseeing coaches, as recognised and approved by the Department of Tourism would be encouraged to ply.

Special Intra-state and Inter-state package tours would be encouraged through private tour operators and travel agents. On nationalised roots RTDC would enter into joint venture with interested parties to manage excursion tours and local sightseeing. RTDC would offer local conducted sight seeing tours at important tourist places in the State.

The Government will initiate steps to ensure charging of standard fares by all surface transport operators from the domestic and international tourists. Prepaid taxi/coach services would be encouraged in the state. There is need to improve the quality of local transport at various tourist destinations. Car taxies for transportation of tourists will be encouraged. Three wheelers will be metered and point to point fixed fare will be introduced to reduce over-charging and harassment to tourists.

Air Services: The State will encourage air taxi service and Helicopter service by air taxi operators within the State so the tourists visiting the State can see as many places as possible within the available time.

There are large number of airstrips and helipads available all over the State. The RTDC in collaboration with the State Department of Civil Aviation and district Collectors would take steps to make use of these air strips and helipads and would motivate Air Taxi Operators (ATO) to undertake special air tours. Private sector investment would be encouraged in setting up airports in Rajasthan. Air Taxi operators (ATOs) would be encouraged to operate civil aviation services for tourists as feeder/ regional airlines.

If necessary RTDC will also take up task of ground handling facilities to encourage ATOs to take up services to Tourist destinations in Rajasthan. RTDC would also explore the feasibility of collaboration with ATOs to promote travel by air. Jaipur Air Port would be developed as an International airport and Ministry of Tourism and Civil Aviation would be requested to allow special tourist charter flights to Jaipur.

In order to increase volume of high spending foreign tourists special charter flights would be encouraged. Collaboration will also be attempted with tourists promotion boards of countries like Singapore for setting up an "air bridge".

TOURIST RECEPTION CENTRES (TRC)

Looking to the large tourist traffic of domestic and international tourists, it becomes increasingly necessary to have modern well-equipped TRC at important entry points and destinations.

Apart from TRCs within the State, at present Skeleton TRCs are functioning at Delhi, Calcutta and Chennai. New TRCs would be started at Mumbai and Bangalore and present TRCs at Delhi, Calcutta and Chennai would be further strengthened and linked by Computer Network.

Apart from offering tourist information, these TRCs would also make available confirmed reservation for RTDC hotels and even for private sector hotels situated within Rajasthan. Information on other details like package tours, fairs and festivals, paying guest accommodation etc. would also be made available at these TRCs. Multimedia software would be developed to provide customised information to tour operators and tourists.

Private Commission Agents will be appointed in other cities to promote tourism from other States. Joint ventures would also be sought with other Tourist Corporations for opening TRCs outside Rajasthan. Joint sector ventures like inter-state packages for tourists will also be attempted with other States and Central Public Sector Corporations, including the Railways, involved in the tourism trade. These TRCs, especially during the tourist season, would be operational for 24 hours in the important tourist places like Delhi, Jaipur, Udaipur Jodhpur, Jaisalmer, Bikaner and Mount Abu.

TOURIST INFORMATION AND PUBLICITY

In order to facilitate dissemination of information to the tourists from foreign and domestic market, the State will cause such literature, films, videos and other material published and produced as is necessary.

A multipronged strategy will be evolved to make optimal use of the media for promoting Rajasthan as an attraction for tourists. Sufficient literature will also be distributed to important Travel Agents and Tour Operators, Air-lines, and Hotel groups for discrimination among important people connected with tourism industry.

High quality tourist literature would be published in foreign languages like French, German, Spanish, Japanese, Italian, Arabic and of course English.

Special efforts would be made for overseas publicity about Rajasthan as a tourist destination. Private marketing and publicity linkages would be established with the help of travel agents and tour operators to promote tourism in Rajasthan in the world tourism market. Special drive would be launched to publicise tourism highlights of Rajasthan in electronic media with the help of e-mail, Internet and latest means of communication available for e-commerce. Efforts would be made to device interactive tourism information packages, CD-ROMs and online reservation facilities for goods and services in tourism sector would be made available in private and public sector.

ENHANCING THE TOURISM PRODUCTS OF RAJASTHAN

Promotion of Handicrafts and Cottage Industries: Rajasthan has a rich and varied heritage of handicrafts, handlooms and other products, which are praised and purchased by tourists visiting the State. Efforts will be made to improve direct access of tourists to artisans who produce these goods to improve their marketing. RTDC will increase shopping arcades in their existing properties and provide space for artisans to display and market their products. Efforts will be made to set-up Shilpgrams at various tourist destinations with assistance of Development Commissioner, Handicrafts, RAJSICO etc. A Handicraft Museum would also be set-up.

HERITAGE TOURISM

The State abounds with some of the best Forts and Palaces in the country spread throughout the State. The Government will encourage the preservation, conservation and upkeep of such heritage properties and selectively open some of them for being developed into Hotels / Tourist Complex.

The State will encourage private investment in developing ancient buildings and heritage properties as tourist resorts. The properties owned by the State government will be offered on easy terms to private entrepreneurs for conversion into hotels. Essential infrastructure, which is considered necessary, would be provided by the State on a selective basis. Corporate sector would be invited to join hands with the Government in conservation of historical heritage and monuments in the State.

Students, Teachers and National Service Scheme (NSS) volunteers would be involved in conservation of monuments.

WEEKEND TOURISM

There is a large segment of tourists from neighbouring areas specially Delhi and Gujarat who visit Rajasthan for weekends. It is proposed to recognise their needs and to provide adequate tourist facilities as also to promote new spots to attract weekend tourists through package tours.

TOURISM AND WILD-LIFE

The State has rich Forest Reserves and National Parks like Sariska, Bharatpur - Ghana and Ranthambhore. The other areas, which have potential for Wildlife tourism, will also be developed for tourism in a planned manner. The Desert Flora and Fauna holds tremendous appeal for the tourists. Special tourists' museum, displaying rich natural and historical heritage of the state would be established in the private and public sector all over the state. Care will be taken to avoid unrestricted entry of tourists beyond the carrying capacity of these National Parks and Sanctuaries. Adverse effect of tourism on the ecosystem would be taken note of and corrective action initiated.

Guides: The importance of trained, well-informed and multilingual guides with proper motivation is very crucial for tourism. It will be the effort of the State to select and train appropriate number of guides at all destinations and tourist circuits within the State.

Department of Tourism would be empowered to select, train and license guides for all destinations and tourist centres within the State. Rajasthan Institute of Tourism and Travel Management (RITTMAN) in collaboration with Universities and Embassies of various important countries functioning at Delhi, would launch special foreign language capsule- courses for guides.

Courses would also be organised for those who are interested in taking up career as language guides, specially in the foreign languages like French, German, Spanish, Italian, Japanese, Chinese, Arabic, English and Indian languages like Bengali and Gujarati.

DOMESTIC TOURISM

Hitherto, most of the attention has been paid in promoting Tourism Centres around Foreign Tourists, with the result that the larger segment of domestic tourism receives secondary attention. It will be the endeavour of the State to take into account the needs of domestic tourists and plan its infrastructure fully keeping in mind this aspect. Special inter state package would be offered for pilgrim tourism by RTDC. Rajasthan is very popular among Gujarati and Bangali tourists. Special efforts will be made to publish tourism literature in Gujarati and Bengali and also launch special packages starting from Ahmedabad and Calcutta to cater to the needs of domestic tourists.

ADVENTURE TOURISM

Suitable Rules/ Guidelines would be framed to provide an enabling legal framework for participation in developing tourism and recreational facilities by the private sector. The State which is predominantly Desert, provides great attraction to foreign and domestic tourists. Most of them have shown preference for activities like Trekking. Horse and Camel Safaris, Polo and Golf. Apart from the Desert, there are numerous Lakes all over the State where Water sports would be developed in a phased manner. Special Water Sport activities like Yachting, Canoeing, Kayaking, Water Sports etc. would be launched in collaboration with the Department of Sports. River cruises would be launched in perennial rivers like Chambal and possibilities of launching Canal Safaris / Canal Cruises in the Indira Gandhi Canal would also be explored in consultation with authorities of Indira Gandhi Nahar Project (IGNP).

Efforts would make to procure Houseboats from the states of Jammu and Kashmir and Kerala and anchor them in big lakes of Rajasthan under the brand name of Palace- On-Waves. These Houseboats would have facades in typically Rajasthan style. These activities will not only provide recreation to the tourists but would also help in extending the period of stay inside the State and would generate lot of employment opportunities for the local residents.

TOURISM POLICY

Mission Statement: A pragmatic policy designed to ensure optimum utilisation of rich tourism resources of the state to generate employmnet specially in rural areas, to develop aready market for the rich and varied handicrafts, to preserve and to accelerate contribution of tourism industry in socioeconomic development of the state by making tourism a truly People's Industry in Rajasthan.

The Preamble: Tourism has emerged as an important instrument for sustainable human development including poverty alleviation, employment generation, environmental regeneration and development of remote areas and advancement of women and other disadvantaged groups in the country apart from promoting social integration and international understanding.

The enunciation of a new pragmatic policy, taking into account the changing socio-economic and investment scenario in the State of Rajasthan and the emerging trends in the tourism phenomenon has thus become necessary.

The primary agenda of Government is to promote tourism as a means to ensure sustainable economic development and positive social change through development of tourism while preserving and protecting the environment and heritage.

Introduction and Present Scenario: With gross out up of US$ 3.4 trillion tourism has emerged as largest and one of the fastest growing industries in the world. Global tax revenue from tourism is estimated at US$ 655 bn (1999). The estimated number of world travellers per annum is over 616 million and these travellers spend over US$ 444 billion as per estimates of World Travel and Tourism Council (WTTC) for year 2000 AD. Every 9th person in the world is engaged in travel & tourism industry for livelihood as per data of World Tourism Organization (WTO). The number of world travellers would go up to 1600 million by the year 2010 AD (WTTC).

Direct employment through the world tourism industry is over 144 million persons (WTTC) and indirect is manifold more. Presently the foreign tourist arrivals in India constitute only about 0.4 percent of the total foreign tourist movement in the world.

One of the objectives of the National Action Plan for tourism announced in May, 1992 by Government of India was to increase India's share in the world tourism market to 1% by 2000 AD (which is still to be achieved). Presently India ranks 44th in the top 60 destinations of the world.

International tourism contributes substantially to foreign

exchange earning. In the year 1999-2000 tourism was the second largest net foreign exchange earner sector for the country, earning Rs.12000 Crores in foreign exchange.

10.6 percent of world's work force is engaged in travel and tourism; tourism contributes 10.2 percent of world's GDP.

In India Travel and Tourism Sector supports 9.3 million jobs and by the year 2010 it would support 12.9 million jobs, thus providing 1 in 15 jobs in the country.

There is a huge domestic tourism market with an estimated 240 million tourists (140 million general tourists and 100 million religious tourists) per annum, spending by them is estimated to be over Rs.95,000 Crores. (Tourism Future Data)

Rajasthan has emerged during the last decade, as one of the favourite tourist destinations in India for both domestic and foreign tourists. While in the year 1973 the total arrivals of tourists to Rajasthan were about 2 million, it has increased to 6.99 million by the year 1998-99.

At present the State receives 0.60 million of the 2.3 million foreign tourists who visit India annually. Additionally over 50 Lacs domestic tourists also visit Rajasthan annually. The world famous "golden triangle" comprising of Delhi-Agra-Jaipur has put Jaipur on the world tourism map. 60% of international tourists visiting India, come to these places.

On an average a foreign tourist spends Rs.800 per day and domestic tourist Rs.400 per day. It is further estimated that the average stay of a foreign tourist in the State is 2.5 days. The total spending by all the tourists visiting the State is over Rs.1000 Crore per annum.

Every rupee spent by a tourist in the State, changes hands thirteen times and every hotel room generate direct employment to three persons and indirectly to eight persons. Rajasthan with its rich historical, cultural and environmental heritage, coupled with colourful fairs and festivals and friendly people has become a favourite destination for tourists from all over the world. Except for a sea-beach and snow-clad mountains, it offers everything to tourists. The rate of growth of tourism in

Rajasthan has been phenomenal in last few years. Annual rate of growth for domestic tourists has been 7% and for international tourists has been 5%. Some of the tourism products of Rajasthan have become internationally famous and popular among the tourists such as Palace-on-Wheels, Heritage Hotels, Camel Safaris, Pushkar Fair, Desert Festival, Palace Hotels and Wild life Sanctuaries/ National Parks.

Recognising the potential attractions that Rajasthan has to offer to domestic and foreign tourists, the Government has accorded Tourism a special status. Tourism was declared industry in Rajasthan in the year 1989.

Objectives

Increase employment opportunities, specially in rural areas for unemployed rural youth.

Optimum utilisation of rich tourist resources of the State in order to attract the maximum number of domestic and international tourists;

To facilitate the growth of tourism in the State and to further involve the private sector in the development of tourism in Rajasthan;

Preservation of rich natural habitat and bio-diversity, historical, architectural and cultural heritage of Rajasthan; special emphasis on conservation of historical monuments in Rajasthan;

To develop a ready market for the rich and varied handicrafts and cottage industries of Rajasthan; ensure welfare of artisans/ artistes;

To promote inter cultural understanding through religious/ pilgrim tourism and fairs and festivals;

To promote socio-economic development of Rajasthan through Tourism with special thrust on backward areas;

To make tourism a "People's Industry" in the state;

To minimise the negative impacts of tourism and promote sustainable tourism;

To open new vistas in tourism like Adventure tourism, Eco-tourism, Camel/Horse safaris, River and Canal cruise, House boats in Rajasthan (Palace-On-Waves), Educational Tourism, Caravan Tourism and Village Tourism.

Jawahar Kala Kendra, Jaipur and other cultural institutions will be associated with Tourism development.

Role of the State Government

1. Catalyst;
2. Promoter, facilitator and providing infrastructure;
3. Pioneer/ Joint Explorer/ Planner;
4. Regulator;
   a. Law and Order;
   b. Tourist Police;
   c. Complaints Handling;
   d. Standaedization of goods and services;
   e. Enactment for Tourism.

Policy Formulation for growth of Tourism Sector

1. Comprehensive Master Plan of State with regional/ sub area/ circuit plans to be updated and executed in a time bound manner;
   1. External assistance;
   2. Central assistance;
   3. State plan resources;
   4. Private sector investment - for a planned development of tourism infrastructure and growth of tourism industry;
2. Growth led by private sector;
3. Developing rural tourism to generate employment in rural areas by launching Paryatan Rozgar Yojana with active participation of Panchayati Raj Institutions (PRIs);
4. Electronic; Print and Cyber Media plan for aggressive marketing of Rajasthan as a premiere tourism destination state;

5. Enhancing and diversifying tourism products of the state;
6. Synergy between tourism and handicrafts, Haat, Shilpgram models to be replicated;
7. State Tourism Advisory Board under the Chairmanship of Chief Minister of Rajasthan constituted to provide policy guidelines.

Ensuring Safety and Security of Tourists and Promoting Sustainable Tourism

1. Alleviation of rural poverty through employment generation by domestic tourism;
2. Tourism to gradually become eco-tourism, responsible tourism;
3. Educating the young ones towards heritage & tourism;
4. Promoting tourism in rural areas;
5. Empowerment of women, improving plight of rural artisans;
6. Making tourist earnings reach the Below Poverty Line threshold in villages;
7. Tourist Police, Safety, Security & hassle free stay of tourists;
8. Tourism regulation, institutional mechanism;
9. Advisory bodies at District, Division and State level;
10. Carrying capacity, code of conduct;
11. HRD, R&D and documentation for Scientific tourism management.

TOURISM INFRASTRUCTURE

The State being the second largest in the country and having perhaps the greatest potential for tourism development, the creation of adequate and suitable infrastructure like accommodation, roads, airport facilities, rail facilities, local transport, communication links and other essential amenities become essential. The Government as well as the private sector shall undertake both the growth of such infrastructure. While the State has to play the leading catalytic role in some sectors, there will be an endeavour to encourage private sector participation in developing infrastructure.

Efforts will be made to dovetail external assistance, central assistance, and State plan resources with private investment to achieve goals set in the Master Plan.

In order to develop infrastructure, the Government will prepare an Area-based Master Plan outlining the infrastructure necessary in each such area. The plan will be based on the potential, which each destination holds for development of Tourism. An investment plan will be evolved from this Master Plan. The Investment Plan will further be translated into an Annual Action Plan in order that the goals set in the Master Plan will be achieved in a time bound manner.

Tourism, by its nature is a multi-sectoral activity, requiring participation of many agencies. Efforts will be made to coordinate these agencies by evolving suitable administrative mechanisms.

Accommodation

The most crucial component for tourism is providing suitable accommodation for various categories of tourists. Since the tourists are not a homogeneous entity, and are highly differentiated; accommodation ranging from budget and economy class to 5 Star and Resorts will have to be augmented.

Rajasthan has estimated tourist accommodation of 19000 rooms in 772 Hotels (DOT.RAJ.) As per requirements estimated by the state department of tourism, 20000 rooms are needed by the year 2007 AD.

The State will endeavour to encourage more private investment in the hotel industry rather than engage itself in raising such infrastructure except in areas where private investment may not be forthcoming.

AJMER—THE LAND OF COMPOSITE CULTURES

Ajmer situated in the green oasis wrapped in the barren hills has been a witness to an interesting past. The city was founded by Raja Ajay Pal Chauhan in the 7th Century A.D. and continued to be a major centre of the Chauhan power till 1193 A.D. when Prithviraj Chauhan lost it to Mohammed Ghauri since then, Ajmer became home to many dynasties, which came and left leaving behind indelible marks of their culture and traditions on the city's history, converting it to an amalgam of various cultures and blend of Hinduism and Islam.

Today, Ajmer is a popular pilgrimage centre for the Hindus as well as Muslims. Especially famous is the Dargah Sharif-tomb of the Sufi saint Khwaja Moinuddin Chisti, which is equally revered by the Hindus and Muslims.

Ajmer is also the base for visiting Pushkar (11 km.), the abode of Lord Brahma, lying to its west with a temple and a picturesque lake. The Pushkar lake is a sacred spot for Hindus. During the month of Kartik (Oct./Nov.), devotes throng in large numbers here to take a dip in the sacred lake.

Prime Sites: The Dargah: At the foot of a barren hill, is situated India's most important pilgrimage centre for people from all faiths. It is the splendid tomb of the Sufi saint Khawaja Moinuddin Chisti more popularly known as Khawaja Saheb or Khawaja Sharif. The shrine is next only to Mecca or Median for the Muslims of south Asia. Akbar used to make a pilgrimage to the Dargah from Agra once a year.

The mausoleum has a gigantic gate, which was built by the Nizam of Hyderabad. The two massive cauldrons in the courtyard are of particular interest and on the right side of the courtyard ins the Akbari Masjid built in white marble. There is another mosque in the courtyard built by Shahjhan.

A View of the Dargah of Khwaja Muinuddin Hasan Chishti, a Sufi Saint

The saint's tomb with a splendid marble dome is in the centre of the second courtyard which is surrounded by a silver platform. The shrine attracts thousands of pilgrims during the Urs-commemorating the death anniversary of the Saint, held from the 1st to 6th day of the Islamic month of Rajab. A colourful fair that springs up during this time is the major attraction.

Shahjhan's Mosque: In the corner of the inner court of the Dargah, is a magnificent building in white marble with a long (30.5m) and narrow court having low arcade and delicate carvings with trellis-work. It is the most marvellous of all the sanctums within the sanctuary of the Dargah.

Adhai-din-ka-jhonpra: A remarkable structure, this is a masterpiece of Indo-Islamic architecture located on the outskirts, of the city, just beyond the Dargah. As the legend goes, its construction took two and a half days (Adhai-Din) to complete. It was originally a Sanskrit college, built within a temple. In 1193 A.D. Mohammed Ghauri conquered Ajmer and converted the building into a mosque by adding a sevenarched wall in front of the pillared hall in just two-and-half days (adhai-din) and hence the name. The distinct pillars-and arched "Screen" with its ruined minarets make it a splendid architectural masterpiece.

Taragarh Fort: A steep one and a half hour climb beyond the Adhai-din-ka-jhopra leads to the ruins of the Taragarh Fort, perched on a hill. One can have an excellent view of the city from here. The fort was the site of the military activity during the Mughal period, later used as a sanatorium by the British

Mayo College: Mayo College has been called the "Eton Of India" since its founding in 1870 AD. This is best expressed in the words of Lord Lytton, Viceroy of India on his visit to Mayo as the Chief Guest on the Annual Prize Giving day on 5th Dec. 1879.

Pushkar Lake (11km.): The lake is situated on the edge of the desert and surrounded by hills on three sides, is separated from Ajmer by 'Nag Pahar'—the snake mountain. On this mountain the Panchkund and the cave of the saint Agastya are located. It is believed that Kalidas-the 4th century sanskrit poet and playright, chose the setting for his masterpiece Abhigyanam Shakuntalam in this forest heritage.

Pushkar Fair: It is one of the most colourful fairs of India. Lakes of pilgrims throng the lake during the annual cattle fair. Besides trading of horses, camels, cows and bulls, there are exciting camel-cart races and cultural events. Cloths, household items and leather goods are for sale during the fair. On the full moon of Kartik (Nov.) pilgrims take a holy dip in the lake.

Man Mahal: Along the banks of the Pushkar Lake is the former residence of Raja Man Singh of Amer, Man Mahal. Presently it is converted to RTDC Sarover Tourist Bungalow ensuring convenient accommodation to travellers. Pushakar palace (Kishangarh House) adjoining it is a heritage hotel.

Foy Sagar (5km) : A picturesque artificial lake named after the engineer for who created it under a famine relief project.

Shopping : Shopping in Ajmer is an enjoyable experience. One can shop for antiques, curios, fascinating gold and silver jewellery in contemporary designs, colourful tie-and-dye sarees and embroidered jodhpuri 'Jutis'. Especially during the annual Urs fair, a range of colourful items and marvellous creations of traditional folk aristsans are for sale.

ALWAR–THE TIGER GATE OF RAJASTHAN

150 Km from Jaipur and 170 Km. From Delhi. Alwar is nested between a cluster of small hills of the Aravali range. Perched on the most prominent of these hills is a massive ancient fort that whispers tales of the rich history of the city.

Once an ancient Rajput state, formerly known as Mewat, Alwar was nearest to the imperial Delhi. The people of the state did not accept any external interference's and daringly resisted against foreign invasions. In the 12th and 13th centuries, they formed a group and raded Delhi. But finally Sultan Bulban (1267 A.D - 1287 A.D) suppressed them, bringing the area under the Muslims rule.

In 1771 A.D. Maharaja Pratap Singh, a Kuchhwaha Rajput belonging to the clan of Jaipur's rulers, won back Alwar and founded a principality of his own.

Apart from its long history, the city has a rich natural heritage with some beautiful lakes and picturesque valleys thickly wooded in parts.

Some of the finest variety of birds and animals are spotted here. Alwar has one of the finest wild life sanctuaries in Rajasthan-Sarika, which is an excellent tiger country.

Prime Sites

The Fort: This huge fort with its ramparts stretching 5 km form north to south and 1.6 km from east to west, stands 304 metres above the city and 595 metres above the sea level. Constructed before the rise of the Mughal empire. Babar had spent a night at this for and took away the hidden treasures to gift to his son, Humayun. Akbar's son, Jahangir had also stayed here for some time during his exile. The place where he stayed is called salim mahal. The for was finally annexed by maharaja Pratap Singh in 1775 A.D. It is a forbidding structure with 15 large and 51 small towers and 446 openings for musketry, along with 8 huge towers encompassing it. The fort has several gates-jai pole, Suraj pole, Laxman Pole, Chand Pole, Kishan Pole and Andheri Gate. Also there are remains of Jal Mahal, Nikumbh Mahal, Salim Sagar, Suraj Kund and many temples.

City Palace or Vinay Vilas Mahal: An 18th century palace harmoniously blending the Rajput and Mughal styles of architecture. While the ground floors have been converted into government offices and district courts, the upper apartment is presently a museum.

Government Museum: The museum has the finest collection of Mughal and Rajput painting dating back to the 18th and 19th centuries and some rare ancient manuscripts in Persian, Arabic, Urdu and Sanskrit. 'Gulistan' (the garden of roses), Waqiat-I-Babri' (autobiography of Mughal emperor Babar) and Bostan (the garden of spring) are some of the notable ones amongst the collection. It also has the copy of the great epic 'Mahabharata' painted by the artists of the Alwar school. A rich collection of the Indian armoury are among other exhibits of the museum. Timings 10.00 hrs. to 17.00 hrs. (closed on Fridays and gazetted holidays. Free entry on Monday.)

Behind the City Palace is an artificial lake built in 1815 A.D. by Maharaja Vinay Singh with few temples along its banks. A marvellous chhatri with unusual Bengali roof and arches, also known as the Moosi Maharani ki chhatri, is situated in this are Purjan Vihar (Company Garden) : A picturesque garden, laid out during the reign of Maharaja Shiv Dan Singh in 1868 A.D. The garden has an enchanting setting called 'Shimla' which was built by Maharaja Mangal Singh in 1885 A.D. The lush surrounding and the cool shades make it the idyllic visiting spot during summers.

Exucrsions

Vijai Mandir Palace (10 km) : A splendid palace, built by Maharaja Jai Singh in 1918 A. D. picturesque lake overlooking the palace makes it a fascinating sight.

A fabulous Sita Ram Temple in the palace attracts number of devotees, especially during Ramnavami. One needs prior permission from the Secretary to visit the palace.

Siliserh Lake Palace Hotel (13 km): An idyllic picnic spot with enchanting landscape of wooded hills and beautiful chhatris on the embankment of the 10.5 sq. km placid lake. A magnificient royal palace and the hunting lodge, built by Maharaja Vinay Singh in 1845 A. D. for his queen Shila stands overlooking the lake. Now converted as the Hotel Lake Palace, it offers boating and sailing facilities and is a delight for the trigger-happy photographers and file makers.

Jai Samand Lake (6 km): A beautiful artificial lake constructed by Maharaja Jai Singh in 1910 A.D. is a popular spot for outing and picnics. During monsoons, sprawling greenery all around makes it a visual treat. Easily accessible by road from Alwar.

Sariska (37 km): The 765.80 sq. km. Thickly wooded reserve cradled in the picturesque valley of the Aravalis. Established in 1955, it is an excellent tiger sanctuary under the Project Tiger. The dry decidous forests of the Reserve are noted for their population of tiger, nilgai, sambhar, cheetal, four horned antelope and wild boar.

Tigers, Sariska Wildlife Sactury: Sariska Palace: A marvellous palace was built here by Maharaja Jai Singh in the honour of the Duke of Edinburgh during his visit to the sancturary. Presently, it has been converted into a hotel- Sariska Palace. RTDC Hotel Tiger Den also offers excellent accommodation at Sariska. The best time to drive in the sanctuary is from till sunset.

BHATRAPUR–THE FAVOURITE BIRD RETREAT

The 55 km journey by road from Agra drives you to the town of Bharatpur-the eastern gateway to Rajasthan. Bharatpur is popular for its bird sanctuary-the Keoladeo Ghana National Park - finest in Asia rich avian variety. Every year the rare Siberian cranes come to spend the winter in the warmer climate of Bharatpur. Of the remnants of the royal past remains the marvellous Bharatpur Palace housing a rich repository of a large number of ancient exhibit that date back to the early 15th century.

Prime Trips

Lohagarh Fort : The massive iron structure built in the early 18th century. With its impregnable defences it sustained itself even after a number of British attacks. The fort was conceived and designed by Maharaja Suraj Mal, the founder of Bharatpur. The fort has three palaces within its precincts - Kishori Mahal, Mahal Khas and Kothi Khas. Government.

Museum : A rich collection of artefacts, exquisitely carved sculptures and ancient inscriptions can be admired in the Government Museum located in the Palaces. All these items speak volumes about the rich heritage, art and crafts of the region.

Deeg Palace

Jawahar Burj and Fateh Burj : A few of the eight

imposing towers still stand erect within the glorious ramparts of the Fort. Especially two of them - Jawahar Burj and Fateh Burj are of special interest. These were built by Maharaja Suraj Mal to commemorate his victories over the Mughals and British respectively.

The coronation ceremony of the Jat rulers of Bharatpur was also help at the Jawahar Burj.

The Palace : This royal edifice is a fusion of the Mughal and Rajpat architectural styles with magnificent apartments and intricately designed floor tiles having interesting patterns. One can marvel at the ancient exhibits displayed in the museum in the central part of the palace

Keoladeo National Park : Once the royal hunting preserve of the princes of Bharatpur, it is one of the finest bird sanctuaries in the world inundated with over 400 species of water birds. Exotic migratory birds from Afghanistan, central. Asia, Tibet as well as Siberian cranes from the arctic, greyleg geese from Siberia and bareheaded geese from China, come here in July/Aug to spend the winters in warmer climate and they breed till Oct/Nov. Colonies of cormorants, spoonbills, storks, egrets, herons, pelicans, ebis and grey herons can be spotted all over the park. The raised paths camouflaged by babul trees make their viewing easier.

Excursions

Deeg (32 km): Once the summer resort of the rulers of Bharatpur, it served as the second capital of the region. This interesting town is strewn with massive fortifications, stunningly beautiful gardens, magnificent palaces and a colourful bazaar.

8

Population and Religion

POPULATION OF RAJASTHAN 2018

Rajasthan is India's biggest state in terms of region. It is located on the north-western part of the country, where it contains a vast part of the wide and intense Thar Desert and borders with the Pakistani region of Punjab and Sindh toward the west. Real components of the state include the remainders of the Indus Valley Civilization at Kalibanga the Dilwara Temples, Mount Abu and other parts.

It was made on 30 March 1949 when Rajputana – the name given by the British Raj for its dependencies in the locale was merged into the Dominion of India. The capital and greatest city is Jaipur, generally called Pink City. Other fundamental urban areas are Udaipur, Bikaner and Ajmer. Rajasthan is notable for its tourist places and consistently many individuals from India and abroad visit this delightful state to have a fabulous time.

Rajasthan is also known for its lip smacking spicy food and the vegetarian flavors can attract anyone with its aroma.

Population Of Rajasthan In 2018:

As per the final of 2011 Census of India, Rajasthan has an aggregate population of 68,548,437. Talking about population, in order to check out the population of Rajasthan in 2018, we need to have a look at the population of the past 5 years. They are as per the following:

1. 2013 – 71.08 Million
2. 2014 – 71.69 Million
3. 2015 – 72.92 Million
4. 2016 – 74.79 Million
5. 2017 – 74.888 Million

Predicting the 2018 population of Rajasthan is not easy but we can get the idea after analysing the population from the year 2013 – 17. As we have seen that every year the population increases by approximate 0.7616 Million people. Hence, the population of Rajasthan in 2018 is forecast to be 74.888 Million + 0.7616 Million = 75.6496 Million. So, the population of Rajasthan in the year 2018 as per estimated data is 75.6496 Million.

Rajasthan Population 2018 –75.6496 Million. (estimated).

Demography Of Rajasthan

Its population is generally made of Hindus, consisting of about 88.45% of the population. Muslims comprise of 9.08%, Sikhs 1.2% and Jains 1%. The state is moreover populated by Sindhis, who came to Rajasthan from Sindh region (now in Pakistan) in the midst of the India-Pakistan partition in 1947. Hindi is the specialist and the most comprehensively spoken dialect in the state, trailed by Bhili(5%) and Urdu (1%).

Population Density And Growth Of Rajasthan

The population density is 165 persons per square kilometre. The number of people in Rajasthan has developed by 21.44% in the latest decade. As indicated by the temporary aftereffects of the Census 2011, it has recorded the eighth highest population growth rate in the country. Be that as it may, the state has recorded a vital fall in the decade growth rate of population.

Facts About Rajasthan:

1. There are equivalent quantities of hues to sarees as there are gatherings of woman grouped together. In addition,

they are taking care of business regarding Fashion, splendid pink, sea blue, brilliant green and so.

2. It is well associated by methods for Roadways, Railways and Airways. It has 3 standard air terminals which are in Jaipur, Udaipur and Jodhpur.
3. People are continually happy to welcome you into their homes and hearts and you are not allowed to go out unless you have water.
4. All the urban areas in Rajasthan are shading composed. Jaipur is pink, Udaipur is shaded white and Jodhpur is blue.
5. We realize that Rajasthan is about sand. Regardless, that is not legitimate. In a couple of parts, you won't see a single spot of desert. There are thick green fields amidst nowhere.

DEMOGRAPHICS

Religion in Rajasthan (2011)

Hinduism (88.49%)

Islam (9.07%)

Sikhism (1.27%)

Jainism (0.91%)

Christianity (0.14%)

Buddhism (0.02%)

Other religions (0.01%)

Not stated (0.10%)

According to final results of 2011 Census of India, Rajasthan has a total population of 68,548,437. The native Rajasthani people make up the majority of the state's population. The state of Rajasthan is also populated by Sindhis, who came to Rajasthan from Sindh province (now in Pakistan) during the India-Pakistan separation in 1947. As for religion, Rajasthan's residents are mainly Hindus, who account for 88.49% of the population. Muslims make up 9.07%, Sikhs 1.27% and Jains 0.91% of the population.

Children performing for Independence Day in village in Alwar district, Rajasthan

Largest cities of Rajasthan by population

City Name	Population
Jaipur	3,073,349
Jodhpur	1,138,300
Kota	1,001,694
Bikaner	647,804
Ajmer	551,101
Udaipur	474,531
Bhilwara	360,009
Alwar	341,422
Bharatpur	252,838
Sri Ganganagar	249,914

Language

Languages in Rajasthan (Census 2001)

Hindi (90.97%)

Bhili (4.60%)

Punjabi (2.01%)

Urdu (1.17%)

Other (1.25%)

Hindi is the official and the most widely spoken language in the state (90.97% of the population as per the 2001 census), followed by Bhili(4.60%), Punjabi (2.01%), and Urdu (1.17%). Rajasthani is one of the main spoken languages in the state. Rajasthani and various Rajasthani dialects are counted under Hindi in the national census. In the 2001 census, standard Rajasthani had over 18 million speakers,as well as millions of other speakers of Rajasthani dialects, such as Marwari. The languages taught under the three-language formula are:

First Language: Hindi

Second Language: English

Third Language: Gujarati, Punjabi, Sanskrit, Sindhi or Urdu

PEOPLE OF RAJASTHAN

According to the census of 2001, the population of Rajasthan is 56.5 million. There is a birth based caste system in Rajasthan. However, the cast system now does not decide the profession of a person, leaving him/her with the career of choice. The people of Rajasthan are divided into various castes and sub-castes. A significant portion of the population of Rajasthan belongs to the Rajput clan. Rajputs were the former rulers of the princely state of Rajasthan. Even today, Rajasthan abounds in the legends of their bravery and chivalry. Rajputs follow the Vedic religion and worship Surya (sun), Lord Shiva and Lord Vishnu. Apart from the predominant Rajputs, the other castes found amongst Rajasthani people are:

Brahmins

Brahmins are a group of priestly people. They have the main occupation of worshipping and performance of religious rites.

Vaishya

The business community is generally referred to as the Vaishyas.

Other Castes

Apart from these castes, there are also a number of agricultural castes in Rajasthan. Depending on agriculture for their livelihood, these people come under the castes Jat, Gurjar, Mali, Kalvi, etc.

A number of tribes, having their own customs and traditions, are found in Rajasthan. Amongst the various tribes of Rajasthan, India, the most known one are:

- Minas/Minawati (found in Alwar, Jaipur, Bharatpur and Dholpur)
- Meo and Banjara (the traveling tribes)
- Gadia Lohar (smiths)
- Bhils (found in Bhilwara, Chittorgarh, Dungarpur, Banswara, Udaipur, and Sirohi)
- Grasia (found in Mewar region)
- Kathodi (found in Mewar region)
- Sahariyas (found in Kota region)
- Rabaris (cattle breeders, found in Marwar region)
- Sansi
- Kanjar.

The most famous community of Rajasthan consists of the Marwaris. Their main occupation relates to trading and business. Marwaris further include the sub castes, namely Mahajans, Sarawagis, Porals, Shrimals, Shrishrimals, Agarwals, Maheswaaris, Vijayvargias, Sunlas, Bohres, Pheriwalas, Baldias and Lohias

RAJASTHAN TRIBES

Rajasthan tribals constitute around twelve percent of the

total population of the state. The tribes of Rajasthan, India constitutes of mainly Bhils and the Minas. Infact, they were the original inhabitants of the area where Rajasthan stands now.

Apart from these main tribes, there are also a number of smaller tribes in Rajasthan. However all Rajasthan tribes share certain common traits, the variations being in their costumes, jewelry, fair and festivals, etc

Here are the main tribes and nomads of Rajasthan:

Bhils

Around 39% of Rajasthan tribals comprises of the Bhils. Dominating in the Banswara area of Rajasthan, the Bhils are believed to be fine archers. Infact, Bhil bowmen even found a reference in the great epics Mahabarata and Ramayan. The Bhils were originally food gatherers. However, with the passage of time, they have taken up small-scale agriculture, city residence and employment. The major festivals of Bhils are the Baneshwar fair (held near Dungarpur) and Holi.

Minas

The second largest tribal group of Rajasthan is that of the Minas. The original inhabitants of the Indus Valley civilization, Minas have a tall, athletic build with sharp features, large eyes, thick lips and a light brown complexion. They are found dominating the regions of Shekhawati and eastern Rajasthan. Minas solemnize marriage in the younger years of the children.

Gadiya Lohars

Gadiya Lohars are wandering blacksmiths that are named after their attractive bullock carts called gadis. Initially a martial Rajput tribe, they left their homeland when Emperor Akbar ousted Maharana Pratap from Chittorgarh.

Garasias

Garasias is a small Rajput tribe inhabiting Abu Road area of southern Rajasthan.

Sahariyas

Sahariyas, the jungle dwellers, is considered as the most backward tribe in Rajasthan. Believed to be of Bhil origin, they inhabit the areas of Kota, Dungarpur and Sawai Madhopur in the southeast of Rajasthan. Their main occupations include working as shifting cultivators, hunters and fishermen.

Damors

Belonging to the Dungarpur and Udaipur districts, Damors are mainly cultivators and manual laborers.

Rajasthan tribes include the following also:

- Meo and Banjara (the traveling tribes)
- Kathodi (found in Mewar region)
- Rabaris (cattle breeders, found in Marwar region)
- Sansi
- Kanjar

RELIGION IN RAJASTHAN

Rajasthanis are predominantly Hindu, Muslims and Jains. However, regardless of their religious segments, Muslim, Hindu and Jain Rajasthanis mingle with each other socially. Most Rajasthani Hindus are *vaishnavas*, however, *Durga* and her avatars are equally worshiped throughout Rajasthan. Oswals are predominantly Jains but small section of vaishnava Oswals are also found. *Jats* are mostly Hindus and Muslims. Meenas of Rajasthan till date strongly follow Vedic culture which usually includes worship of *Bhainroon* (Shiva) and *Krishna* as well as *Durga*. The *Rajputs* generally worship the Sun, Lord Shiva, Lord Vishnu and Bhavani (Goddess *Durga*). The Gurjars (Gujars or Gujjars) worship the Sun God, God Devnarayan, Lord Vishnu, Lord Shiva and Goddess Bhavani. Historically, The Gurjars were Sun-worshipers and are described as devoted to the feet of the Sun-god. Marathi *Bhakti* movement by Mahanubbavis and Virakaripanthis of Maharashtra had immense influence on the development of *Rajasthani Bhakti* movement. Meerabai was an important figure during 'Rajasthani Bhakti*movement.*

Rajasthani Muslims are predominantly Sunnis. They are mainly Khan, Meo, Syed, Mirasi, Mughals, Qaimkhani, Neelgar, Manganiar, Muslim Rangrez, Bohra, Merat, Sheikh, Qureishi, Ansaari, Qazi, Sindhi-Sipahi, Rath and Pathans.

With the introduction of Islam, some communities converted to Islam, though pre-Islamic community identity and many pre-Islamic socio-ritual elements have persisted. Rajasthani Muslim communities, after their conversion, continued to follow pre-conversion practices (Rajasthani rituals and customs) which is not the case in other parts of the country.

This exhibits the strong cultural identity of Rajasthani people as opposed to religious identity.

Some other religions are also prevalent such as Buddhism, Christianity, Parsi religion etc. Over time, there has been an increase in the number of followers of Sikh religion. Though Buddhism emerged as a major religion during 321-184 BC in *Mauryan Empire*, it had no influence in Rajasthan for the fact that Mauryan Empire had minimal impact on Rajasthan and its culture. Although, today Jainism is not that prevalent in Rajasthan but historically Rajasthan and Gujarat areas were strong centres of Jainism in India.

Hinduism

Of all the Rajasthan religions, the predominant one is Hinduism. This religion consists in the worship of Brahma, Shiva, Shakti, Vishnu, and other gods and goddesses. Along with Hinduism, there is also Arya Samaj (a reforming sect of modern Hinduism). Some of the famous Hindu religious places in Rajasthan are - Nathdwara, Eklingji Shiva Temple, Birla Mandir (temple), Govind Devji Temple, Brahma Temple and so on.

Islam

The expansion of Islam in Rajasthan started with the conquest of Ajmer by Muslim invaders in the late 12th century. Ajmer was, in fact, the headquarters of Khwajah Moin-ud-Din

Salim Chishti, the Muslim missionary. There is also his famous dargah in Ajmer, known as "Chishti ki Dargah"

Jainism

Another important and widely followed religion in Rajasthan is Jainism. The main followers of this religion include the trading class and the wealthy section of society. The famous religious places of Jains in Rajasthan include Ossian Jain Temples, Dilwara Jain Temples, Ranakpur Jain Temple and so on.

Dadupanthi

Another religious sect of Rajasthan includes the Dadupanthis. They are the followers of Dadu, who preached the equality of all men, strict vegetarianism, total abstinence from intoxicating liquor, and lifelong celibacy.

Sikhism

Over the years, the number of Sikhs in Rajasthan has increased to a considerable extent.

Christians

The population of Christians in Rajasthan is quite small.

9

Art, Architecture, Fair and Festivals

RAJASTHAN ARTS AND CRAFTS

Rajasthan is well known all over the world for its hand-printed textiles, furniture, leatherwork, jewellery, painting, pottery and metal craft.

The use of lively colors and flamboyant, fantasy designs is distinctive in all forms of arts and crafts of Rajasthan.It will be unfair to say that Rajasthani artists only make decorative items. Every household item in Rajasthan proves the statement false as we go through their embellished utensils, colorful attires, unique jewellery designs and embroidered shoes that infuse a new life and a cheerful look to the otherwise monotone of the desert sands.

Carpets and Dhurries

Floor coverings like carpets, hand-woven durries and namdas or soft woollen druggets of Rajasthan are exported all over the world. Available in all sizes, the dhurrie is woven in Jaipur and also in the rural areas of the state. Bikaner and Jaisalmer are known for woolen dhurries made of camel hair. Bikaner is also famous for its so-called jail carpets, which are so called for they were once made by the prisoners in the medieval times. Much like Persian carpets, Rajasthani hand-knotted carpets have geometric motifs and formal designs with a border and central motif. The motifs have indeed been localized and include peacocks and other local icons. Jaipur and Bikaner are believed to be the pioneer centres in carpet weaving.

Antiques: Not all of the items in the handicrafts shop that you find in Rajasthan can exactly pass off as antiques of course but still their distinctive color and designs make them popular among the tourists who buy them as souvenirs and as decorative items for their homes. The large iron oil jars painted in the pichwai style, depicting the love scenes, are just an example. Similarly, variety of kitchen utensils, votive objects and even camel saddles attract attention of the visitors.

Fabrics: Printed, dyed or embroidered fabrics of Rajasthan are known for their unique hues and tones of color. Block printing, batik, tie and dye has become a full-fledged artwork here. Each region has its own distinct motifs, choice of colors, and the way in which these colors are used. Bagru is known for earth colors and geometric patterns while Sanganeri clothes have bright colors and floral patterns. Barmer and Jaisalmer are famous for their batik or reverse printing work. Sikar and Jodhpur are famous for intricate tie-and-dye or bandhani designs including chunari (dotted), lahariya (diagonal striped waves) and mothra (large dots) prints. Bikaner, Sikar and Jhunjhunu are well known for the mirror work, embroidery and appliqué work that are used to embellish these fabrics to produce elaborate designs of Rajasthani dresses.

Furniture and wood carving: Rajasthan is an ideal place to look for old-worldly doors and windows, wooden jharokhas, tables with cast iron jaalis, side-boards, chairs, benches, jhoolas or swings and dressers, sometimes fretted with brass and copper sheets for decoration. They can be lightly carved or embellished with tiles. Jaipur and Ramgarh in Shekhawati are popular centers for furniture but Jodhpur gets the first place. The notable places are Shekhawati and Bikaner for traditional woodwork, Jodhpur and Kishangarh for painted wooden furniture, Shekhawati, Bikaner and Ramgarh for delicately carved wooden doors, Barmer for woodcarvings such as images of gods and goddesses, elephants, parrots, human and animal figures, Tilonia for leather-embroidered chairs of Tilonia and Shekhawati for carved-back, string-bottom chairs. The most remarkable and finest type of artwork belongs to Bikaner. Known as Gesso work, it is made using the inner hide of the camel, which is scraped till it is paper-thin and translucent and is then molded into various forms of lampshades, hip flasks, perfume phials or vases.

Pottery: The different regions of Rajasthan have distinctive style of pottery. Jaipur is famous for its blue glazed pottery that doesn't use simple clay but ground quartz stone, fuller's earth and sodium sulphate.Terra-cotta pottery is also quite popular in Rajasthan. Molela, a village near Udaipur is specialized in making clay images of deities for ceremonial occasions. Alwar is known for its paper-thin pottery while Bikaner's painted pottery is tinted with lac colors. The white and red clay articles of Pokaran are marked with distinct geometric designs.

Leather ware: In Rajasthan, jootis (the embroidered footwear the people wear), saddles, bags and pouches are not the only objects made out of animal skins. The other uses to which they are commonly put are making backs of chairs embroidered with woolen motifs. The leather is beaten, tanned and dyed and patterns are made on it by punching and gouging it. Later it is studded and sequined for effect, and embroidered and stitched to create the special jootis (slip-on shoes) that have become a style-statement. Jaipur and Jodhpur are famous for these 'jootis'.

Metal Crafts: Started off with embellishing the royal armor, the metal crafts of Rajasthan now adorn tabletops, wall plates, flasks, silver animal figures, caparisoned elephants with human figures over a howdah (a musical instrument). Jaipur, Alwar and Jodhpur are famous for their metal wares such as brassware and enameled, engraved and filigree cutwork on silver.

Paintings: Miniature paintings, portraits, courtly paintings, murals, paintings on cloth and furniture, henna body art, domestic paintings and mandana (the art of decorating houses) are just of the various form of vibrantly colored and intricate Rajasthani paintings.Mostly the paintings depict scenes from Ramayana, Krishna Lila and the Gita Govindam and use rich colors that were made using minerals, vegetables, precious stones, conch shells and metals like gold and silver. Jaipur, Jodhpur, Nathdwara and Kishangarh are important centers of such paintings. Other remarkable styles are phads or scrolls with the tales of the folk-hero Pabuji and the pichwais of Nathdwara near Udaipur, that depict scenes from the with life of Lord Krishna and are often decorated with precious stones.

Puppets: Painted wooden heads, hands made simply by stuffing rags or cotton into the sleeve of the dress, with painted expressions, arched eyebrows, mustache for men and nose ring for women and large expressive eyes on their face, puppets are draped with dresses made from sequined old fabrics. They are extremely popular as inexpensive mementos among the tourists.

Stone Carving: The forts and palaces and beautiful havelis of Rajasthan are all superb examples of the exquisite mason work of the state. Dholpur near Bharatpur and Barmer are popular for panels of frescoes for buildings, large statuaries, planters, and intricately carved elephants and horses as garden sculptures. White marble statues of deities are considered to be a specialty of Jaipur.

HISTORY OF ARTS AND CRAFTS IN RAJASTHAN

Each period of history had some stroke of ingenuity to contribute to the aesthetic heritage of this land. The kings and nobles were lovers of arts and crafts and encouraged craftsmen in their activities. Art flourished in this region as far back as 2nd-1st centuries BC and continued over the centuries. In Baroli, in the Hadoti region, presence of several sculptures proves that a regular art school existed in the 10th century. The cave paintings, terracotta and other stone sculptures excavated at different sites corroborate this.

Each period of history saw its own contribution to the thriving art scene. History of Rajasthan reveals that the kings and their nobles were patrons of arts and crafts and they encouraged their craftsmen in activities ranging from wood and marble carving to weaving, pottery and painting. And art seems to have been an obsession with the inhabitants of this parched landscape. The desire to decorate their surroundings was very strong. Nothing was overlooked animals from the regal elephant to the lowly donkey, the great palaces and the inner chambers of forbidding forts were decorated with as much attention as were the walls of humble mud huts. The inhabitants were not too far behind when it came to adorning themselves and it was not only the women who beautified themselves the heroic warriors extended equal attention to their clothing and armour they went into battles with meticulously ornamented swords and shields. The horses and elephants that took the warriors to battles received the same care jeweled saddles and intricate silver howdas were just some of the ornaments that were used to adorn them.

For women in Rajasthan, there was infinite variety tie and dye fabrics, embroidered garments, enamel jewellery inlayed with precious and semi-precious stones, leather jootis. They put their lives indoors to very good use by decorating their surroundings on the walls of their mud-huts were painted geometric designs as well as simple designs like flowers and birds. Also tile women folk made intricate patterns outdoors, shaped straw and twine to turn into the most beautiful items.

When the Rajputs came to dominate this region, it was a period of constant strife. They were almost always in battle with their neighbouring kingdoms. When a kingdom fell and a new ruler took over, it was time for change of paintings to the one's depicting the new ruler's victory, scenes from the battle and processions of the victorious march were faithfully reproduced on the walls and handmade paper. Other than the paintings, the new rulers also influenced the existing crafts of that area. Despite their love for the battlefield, the Rajputs have been patrons of art and also their 350 years of contact with the Mughals led to a very strong influence on their lives and arts. Quite a few folk arts received the refinement and delicacy of the Mughal courts. They borrowed freely from the Agra and Delhi courts and in some cases, also sent their skilled craftsmen to adorn the Mughal courts.

Rajasthan is well known all over the world for its hand-printed textiles, furniture, leatherwork, jewellery, painting, pottery and metal craft. The use of lively colors and flamboyant, fantasy designs is distinctive in all forms of arts and crafts of Rajasthan. It will be unfair to say that Rajasthani artists only make decorative items. Every household item in Rajasthan proves the statement false as we go through their embellished utensils, colorful attires, unique jewellery designs and embroidered shoes that infuse a new life and a cheerful look to the otherwise monotone of the desert sands. Some of the popular crafts are mentioned below.

Carpets and Dhurries of Rajasthan

Floor coverings like carpets, hand-woven durries and namdas or soft woollen druggets of Rajasthan are exported all over the world. Available in all sizes, the dhurrie is woven in Jaipur and also in the rural areas of the state of Rajasthan. Bikaner and Jaisalmer are known for woolen dhurries made of camel hair. Bikaner is also famous for its so-called jail carpets, which are so called for they were once made by the prisoners in the medieval times. Much like Persian carpets, Rajasthani hand-knotted carpets have geometric motifs and formal designs with a border and central motif. The motifs have indeed been localized and include peacocks and other local icons. Jaipur and Bikaner of Rajasthan are believed to be the pioneer centres in carpet weaving.

Antiques of Rajasthan

Not all of the items in the handicrafts shop that you find in Rajasthan can exactly pass off as antiques of course but still their distinctive color and designs make them popular among the tourists who buy them as souvenirs and as decorative items for their homes. The large iron oil jars painted in the pichwai style, depicting the love scenes, are just an example. Similarly, variety of kitchen utensils, votive objects and even camel saddles attract attention of the visitors.

Ivory Carving of Rajasthan

Rajasthan has its main ivory carving centres at Udaipur, Bharatpur and Jaipur from where master ivory carvers were once favoured by the royal courts. While Jaipur was famous for its carved ivory, Jodhpur specialized in ivory bangles. The bangles were worn to cover the whole arm and they decreased in size from just below the shoulder to the wrist. The Bikaner Palace is well known and prominent for its artistic ivory inlaid doors than the palace itself. Carved ivory artifacts can be purchased in and around Jaipur but the export of ivory in any form from India is strictly banned.

Shellac Bric-a-Brac of Rajasthan

Brightly coloured lac bangles, handmirrors, pens, pillboxes and agarbatti (incense) stands are a cheerful and inexpensive buy in Rajasthan. In the pink city of Jaipur, lac trinkets are a common sight in every bazaar. Check out the dazzling bangles, often studded with glass gems, spirals of base-metal wire amid a wavy striping of other colours of Rajasthan.

Fabrics of Rajasthan

Printed, dyed or embroidered fabrics of Rajasthan are known for their unique hues and tones of color. Block printing, batik, tie and dye have become a full-fledged artwork here. Each region has its own distinct motifs, choice of colors, and the way in which these colors are used. Bagru is known for earth colors and geometric patterns while Sanganeri clothes have bright colors and floral patterns. Barmer and Jaisalmer are famous for their batik or reverse printing work. Sikar and Jodhpur are famous for intricate tie-and-dye or bandhani designs including chunari (dotted), lahariya (diagonal striped waves) and mothra (large dots) prints. Bikaner, Sikar and Jhunjhunu are well known for the mirror work, embroidery and appliqué work that are used to embellish these fabrics to produce elaborate designs of Rajasthani dresses.

Bandhani or Tie and Dye of Rajasthan

As the name suggests, this technique involves two stages: tying sections of a length of cloth (silk or cotton) and then dunking it into vats of colour. The rainbow-tinged turbans of the Rajputs and the odhnis of their women are shaded by this method of resist dyeing. Your visit to Jaipur won't be complete without a trip to the nearby towns of Bagru and Sanganer, where you can observe the Chhipa community of dyers at work.

The main colours used in Bandhani are yellow, green, red and black. It is essentially a household craft supervised by the head of the family. The fabric is skillfully knotted by the women, while the portfolio of dyeing rests with the men. The women often grow a long nail on the little finger of the left hand, or wear a ring with a little blunt spike on it, with which they push the cloth upwards to form a tiny peak.

The Jaipur dyer of Rajasthan rarely works with more than two dye baths while the additional colours are spot dyed, which makes the process much easier. Thereafter, the fabric opens out into amazing designs in kaleidoscopic colours: dots, circles, squares, waves and stripes. The laheriya or the ripple effect is achieved by a variation of this technique. Lengths of permeable muslin are rolled diagonally from one corner to the opposite, bound tightly at intervals and then dyed. The ties are then undone and the process repeated by diagonally rolling the adjacent corner toward the opposite and repeating the process. Both Jaipur and Jodhpur are major centres of laheriya. Jaipur in particular, thanks to its status as the state capital, has girt its loins to meet the extensive demands of both the domestic and export markets.

Tie and dye cloth is never too expensive but be warned that the colours always run. So if you've bought silk, it's safer to get it dry-cleaned.

Block-printing of Rajasthan

Rajasthan has a long and distinguished traditon of printing with finely carved wooden blocks. What you might have already seen in Delhi's Rajasthali or Fabindia is merely the tip of the iceberg. Head for Bagru and Sanganer, not far from Jaipur, to see for yourself how cloth is printed by hand.

This method, though labourious, is actually quite simple and merely calls for precision. The cloth is laid out flat on a table or bench and a freshly dipped block is handpressed on to the fabric to form a continuous, interlocking pattern. The block carries dye if the original colour of the cloth has to be preserved. If the cloth has to be dyed, the block is used to apply an impermeable resist – a material such as clay, resin or wax – to demarcate the pattern that is not to be coloured. Later, when the cloth is dyed, the pattern emerges in reverse. Traditonally, block-printing relied on the use of natural dyes and pigments, but now synthetic dyes have gained currency as they are cheaper. If you belong to the green brigade, stick to eco-friendly naturally dyed cloth.

The floral motifs favoured by the printers of Bagru and Sanganer are Persian in origin, though Sanganeri designs are more sophisticated. They usually have a white or pale background decorated with colorful twigs or sprays. The not-so-fine Bagru prints were initially meant for peasants and had a light brown background. Today, however, Bagru isn't the poor second cousin any more.

Block-printed cloth is sure to fade too after a few washes. Once again, stick to drycleaning.

Zari, Gota, Kinari & Zardozi of Rajasthan

Zari is gold, and zardozi embroidery of Rajasthan is the glitteringly ornate, heavily encrusted gold thread work practiced in Jaipur and a few other cities of India. To most foreigners - used to sleek, understated wear - the north Indian bride's lehanga, choli and dupatta, heavily emroidered with gold and silver threads comes as a visual shock. Either real silver thread, gold-plated thread or an imitation which has a copper base gilded with gold or silver colour is used for zari.

Traditionally made for Mughal and Rajput nobility, it has now been officially adopted as bridal wear by anyone who can afford it. Of course, the days of using real gold and silver thread are now history. What you can get, however, is synthetic or 'tested' zari embroidery. Metal ingots are melted and pressed through perforated steel sheets, to be converted into wires. They are then hammered to the required thinness. Plain wire is called badla, and when wound round a thread, it is called kasav.

Smaller spangles are called sitara, and tiny dots made of badla are called mukaish.

Akin to applique, gota work involves placing woven gold cloth onto other fabric to create different surface textures. Kinari, or edging, as the word suggests, is the fringed or tasselled border decoration. This art is predominantly practised by Muslim craftsmen.

Zardozi, a more elaborate version of zari, involves the use of gold threads, spangles, beads, seed pearls, wire, gota and kinari. Zardozi work makes a garment quite heavy so do try it on before buying. Besides, the metal thread work can make your skin feel itchy, see if you can handle that.

Jewellery of Rajasthan

Rajasthan is rich in jewellery, each area having its own unique style. Some of the traditional designs are rakhri, bala, bajuband, gajra, gokhru, jod, etc. tribal women wear heavy, simply crafted silver jewellery. Men also wear ornaments in the form of chockers and earrings. During Mughal Empire, Rajasthan became a major centre for production of fine kind of jewellery. It was a true blend of the Mughal with the Rajasthani craftsman ship. The Mughals brought sophisticated design and new technical know-how of the Persians origin with them.

Silver Jewellery of Rajasthan

Traditionally, jewellery of Rajasthan has served as a repository of wealth, and a bejeweled wife is the family's walking-talking treasury. While the prince had his gold, the peasant found security in silver. The village women of Rajasthan are togged up from head to toe in cumbersome silver ornaments, which they never remove.

The various kinds of adornments they use are: tikka or the spherical pendant on the forehead; dangling earrings called jhumkas; hansli or the choker; nath or the nosering which may be attached with a chain to the adjacent jhumka; a girdle or taqri for the waist; a series of bracelets called kadas; anklets with tiny bells on them; and finally the chakti or toe rings of the married women of Rajasthan.

Not to be outdone, the masculine jewellery is as much a part of Rajasthani culture as the feminine jewellery. The turbans worn by men are heavily encrusted with jewels and fastened with a gem set kalangi or aigrette.

The ornament worn in front of the turban is called a sarpech. It was often extended into a golden bank set with emeralds, rubies or diamonds. Pearls were greatly loved by the Maharajas and they often wore double or triple strings of pearls with pendant of precious stones round their necks.

Men also wore earrings, jeweled sashes around their waists and several rings on every finger. It was a status symbol and a portable display of wealth, and consequently, power. Earrings, armlets and anklets of silver are still commonly seen adorning the rural Rajasthani male. Males also wear necklaces, earrings and lucky charms which are considered to ward off evil.

In Jaipur, you'll find silver jewellery makers and exporters near the Badi Chaupad in Johari Bazaar. Ornate tribal designs, geometric patterns and filigree work are much in demand. A relatively new addition to the repertoire is silver studded with semi-precious stones. Apart from jewellery, you'll also find little silver boxes, statuettes, containers, glasses, plates, bowls, pens, hand mirrors and gilt combs.

Silver is often alloyed with other metals before being made into ornaments. So beware of silversmiths who mix more than the required amount.

Gems, Kundan and Meenakari Jewellery of Rajasthan

If you are searching for a quality diamond or emerald Jaipur is just the place for you. What's more, if you believe in the occult, you can even find jyotshis (palmists and astrologers) to dig out your lucky stone. They'll tell you precisely the clarity and carats required to ward off the evil eye or reverse a spell of ill luck. The Pink City is known for its vast array of precious and semi-precious stones, running the gamut from diamond, emerald, sapphire and ruby to topaz, jade, garnet, amethyst and turquoise. The craft of cutting and polishing stones to achieve the most gleaming facets has been honed to perfection. Watch the craftsmen at work in Johari Bazaar.

Moving from gems, the next stage is obviously transforming them into exquisite jewellery. Bengali craftsmen, who settled in Jaipur centuries ago, are the acknowledged masters. The two special techniques practised in Jaipur – kundan and meenakari – are equally intricate and splendid, and it is impossible to say which outshines the other.

Kundan is the Mughal-inspired art of setting of stones in gold and silver. Gems are bedded in a surround of gold leaf rather than secured by a rim or claw.

Hindu Punjabis brought Meenakari, or the skill of enamelling, from Lahore to Jaipur. Did you know that enamelling was originally meant to protect gold, which in its pure state is so soft and malleable that it can easily wear away? The Mughal fashion was to enamel the reverse side of jewellery to protect it from contact with the wearer's skin.

Enamelling is a champleve technique, which in simple English means that a recess is hollowed out in the surface of gold or silver to take in a mineral.

For example, cobalt oxide, which gives a blue colour, is then fired into the depression so as to leave a thin line separating the segments of colour.

You can observe jewellers doing the enamel work at the Jadiyon ka Rasta in Jaipur. An ornament with both kundan and meenakari is so astoundingly magnificent that it seems to have been conjured up by rubbing Aladdin's magical lamp.

Ivory of Rajasthan

Ivory is often used to make jewellery, especially bangles, which are considered an essential part of bridal jewellery. The bangles are often over laid with gold. They are often dyed in various colors, though the most popular one is red. Ivory is also inlaid and shaped into intricate items of great beauty. Miniature paintings were also executed on the ivory.

Lac and Glass of Rajasthan

Lac is mainly used bangles and decorative items. Lac bangles are made in bright colours. These bangles and decorative items are inlaid with glass and coloured stone.

Rajasthan is rich in jewellery, each area having its own unique style. Some of the traditional designs are rakhri, tirnaniyan, bala, bajuband, gajra, gokhru, jod, etc. Tribal women wear heavy, simply crafted jewellery and seem to carry the weight (almost up to five kgs) without much discomfort almost all the time. Men too wear their share of ornaments in the form of chockers and earrings.

Furniture and wood carving of Rajasthan

Rajasthan is an ideal place to look for old-worldly doors and windows, wooden jharokhas, tables with cast iron jaalis, side-boards, chairs, benches, jhoolas or swings and dressers, sometimes fretted with brass and copper sheets for decoration. They can be lightly carved or embellished with tiles. Jaipur and Ramgarh in Shekhawati are popular centers for furniture but Jodhpur gets the first place. The notable places are Shekhawati and Bikaner for traditional woodwork, Jodhpur and Kishangarh for painted wooden furniture, Shekhawati, Bikaner and Ramgarh for delicately carved wooden doors, Barmer for woodcarvings such as images of gods and goddesses, elephants, parrots, human and animal figures, Tilonia for leather-embroidered chairs of Tilonia and Shekhawati for carved-back, string-bottom chairs. The most remarkable and finest type of artwork belongs to Bikaner. Known as Gesso work, it is made using the inner hide of the camel, which is scraped till it is paper-thin and translucent and is then molded into various forms of lampshades, hip flasks, perfume phials or vases.

Pottery of Rajasthan

The different regions of Rajasthan have distinctive style of pottery. Jaipur is famous for its blue glazed pottery that doesn't use simple clay but ground quartz stone, fuller's earth and sodium sulphate.Terra-cotta pottery is also quite popular in Rajasthan. Molela, a village near Udaipur is specialized in making clay images of deities for ceremonial occasions. Alwar is known for its paper-thin pottery while Bikaner's painted pottery is tinted with lac colors. The white and red clay articles of Pokaran are marked with distinct geometric designs.

Jaipur Blue Pottery of Rajasthan

The art of making blue glaze pottery came to Rajasthan via Kashmir, the Mughal emperors' favourite retreat and, more importantly, their entry point into India. The use of blue glaze on pottery made from Multani mitti, or Fuller's earth, is essentially an imported technique, first developed by enterprising Mongol artisans who combined Chinese glazing technology with Persian decorative arts. This technique travelled south to India with early Muslim potentates in the 14th century. During its infancy, it was strictly used to make tiles to decorate mosques, tombs and palaces in Central Asia.

Later, the Mughals began using them in India, in a bid to mimic their beloved structures from beyond the mountains in Samarkand. Gradually the blue glaze technique broke free of its status as an architectural accessory, and Kashmiri potters took to it with a vengeance. From there, the technique rolled down to the plains of Delhi and in the 17th century wound its way to Jaipur. The rulers of Jaipur were exceptionally partial to blue-glazed ware, and many a cool marble hall in Rambagh Palace has as its centrepiece a bubbling fountain lined with ravishing blue tiles. These tiles were also used extensively in the building of the splendid city of Jaipur but surprisingly, they disappeared soon after.

The revival of tile-making began in the late 19th century, and Jaipur became the centre of a thriving new industry producing blueware. The traditional Persian designs have now been adapted to please a more sophisticated clientele. Apart from the predictable urns, jars, pots and vases, you'll now find tea sets, cups and saucers, plates and glasses, jugs, ashtrays and even napkin rings. You can spot blue pottery being made at Sanganer, not far from Jaipur, and also within the city at Kripal Kumbh, Shiva Marg. The colour palette is restricted to blue derived from the oxide of cobalt, green from the oxide of copper and white, though other non-conventional colours such as yellow and brown have jumped into the fray too.

Leather ware of Rajasthan

In Rajasthan, jootis (the embroidered footwear the people wear), saddles, bags and pouches are not the only objects made out of animal skins. The other uses to which they are commonly put are making backs of chairs embroidered with woolen motifs. Leather is also used for bookbinding and Alwar is well reputed for this craft that flourished in the 19th century under Maharaja Banni Singh. Bikaner is again famous for its kopis or camel-hide water bottles.

The leather is beaten, tanned and dyed and patterns are made on it by punching and gouging it. Later it is studded and sequined for effect, and embroidered and stitched to create the special jootis (slip-on shoes) that have become a style-statement. Jaipur and Jodhpur are famous for these 'jootis'. Embroidery known as kashida is done on the jootis: in Jaipur it is first done on velvet which is then made to cover the shoes while in Jodhpur it is applied directly to the leather. This embroidery is mainly done by the women, who also do a bit of fancy stitching or appliqué work to give a designer look to the shoes that have neither a left nor a right foot.

Metal Crafts of Rajasthan

Started off with embellishing the royal armor, the metal crafts of Rajasthan now adorn tabletops, wall plates, flasks, silver animal figures and caparisoned elephants with human figures over a howdah (a musical instrument). Jaipur, Alwar and Jodhpur are famous for their metal wares such as brassware and enameled, engraved and filigree cutwork on silver.

Tarkashi of Rajasthan

A common sight in the curio and gift shops of Jaipur is boxes, tables and trays with brass or copper inlay work. This type of work is called tarkashi and it utilises burnished metal wire or tar set in the wood to create delicate geometric patterns. Deeper, in the narrow alleyways of the city, you can locate master craftsmen at work.

Onto a plain, dark shisham surface, a naqsha (map) of the design is glued. The outline is then incised into the wood with a small chisel.

The worker cuts 2 mm ribbons from a sheet of brass or copper, tempers them and then, placing one on edge in an incised line, he hammers it until it is level with the surface. The metal comes in various gauges, the thickest being used for strong outlines, and the finest for details such as hair. A lick of polish and varnish, and the object is ready for sale.

Paintings of Rajasthan

Miniature paintings, portraits, courtly paintings, murals, paintings on cloth and furniture, henna body art, domestic paintings and mandana (the art of decorating houses) are just of the various form of vibrantly colored and intricate Rajasthani paintings.Mostly the paintings depict scenes from Ramayana, Krishna Lila and the Gita Govindam and use rich colors that were made using minerals, vegetables, precious stones, conch shells and metals like gold and silver. Jaipur, Jodhpur, Nathdwara and Kishangarh are important centers of such paintings. Other remarkable styles are phads or scrolls with the tales of the folk-hero Pabuji and the pichwais of Nathdwara near Udaipur that depict scenes from the life of Lord Krishna and are often decorated with precious stones.

Wall Painting of Rajasthan

Palaces, Havelies, even huts are commonly having Walls and ceilings covered with colourful paintings in Rajasthan. Some of the finest paintings can be seen in havelis of the Shekhawati region and the ancient towns of Bundi and Kota. And some of the most humorous on the walls of houses tucked away in the lanes of Jaisalmer.

Cloth Paintings of Rajasthan

They include the phad and the pichwai (cloth hanging used behind the deity in Vaishnava temples such as the temple of Shrinathji at Nathdwara). Done in bright colours with bold outlines, these paintings have strong religious traditions.

Miniature Paintings of Rajasthan

A host of schools of miniature painting thrive in Rajasthan and, to a certain extent; they are a quaint mixture of Mughal and indigenous Indian styles. The Indian style dates back to the Jain manuscripts of western India, now preserved in the temples of Rajasthan and Gujarat. These manuscripts are inscribed on palm leaves and are illustrated with stylized miniatures, elements of which are obvious in the miniatures of today. If you examine these miniatures from the 11th century, you'll find that the human forms are far from proportionate as the figures were squeezed in to fit the long, narrow format of the leaves. Fortunately with the coming of paper in the 12th century (thanks to the Arab traders), the miniatures were freed from this constraint.

Anyway, the long and short of it was that this style merged happily with the opulent Mughal court style and several distinct schools of Rajasthan miniatures were born: the Mewar or Udaipur school, the Bundi school, the Kishangarh school, the Bikaner school, the Jaipur school and the Alwar school. It seems that every little Rajput fiefdom worth its name encouraged its own unique style. The verdant greenery of the Kota-Bundi region is reflected in the paintings of that region.

The rulers of Amer-Jaipur were the closest to the Mughals and a strong Mughal influence crept into their paintings. Fierce camel fights; bejewelled women stretching seductively or in various stages of undress; midnight trysts of the divine lovers Radha and Krishna; Krishna painting a delicate tattoo on the breast of his sweetheart, Radha; the blood and gore of a tiger or boar hunt; the amorous dalliances of Rajput princes and the pomp and ceremony of the Mughal court - Rajasthani miniatures unabashedly celebrate every aspect of life. The paintings are a rich reminder of how both the regal Mughals and the proud Rajputs lived life in bold Technicolor.

In the back streets of the Pink City, you'll find Brahmin artists working on a variety of materials from handmade paper and boards of wood to ivory and marble. Most of them still use natural colours derived from insects, shells, minerals, vegetable matter as well as silver and gold. Using the finest squirrel hairbrushes, it takes miniaturist weeks to complete a commission. Their lack of originality – most of them merely replicate the work of their forefathers – is more than compensated for by their breathtakingly precise and detailed workmanship. Sadly, some of the more sales oriented artists have now switched to cheaper chemical colours to satisfy the demand of tourists.

Miniature paintings were once made on a base of ivory but that's all in the past. The use of ivory has been banned now in the interests of our wildlife. So don't get conned into buying an ivory painting or artifact.

Puppetry in Rajasthan

Painted wooden heads, hands made simply by stuffing rags or cotton into the sleeve of the dress, with painted expressions, arched eyebrows, mustache for men and nose ring for women and large expressive eyes on their face, puppets are draped with dresses made from sequined old fabrics. They are extremely popular as inexpensive mementos among the tourists.

Stone Carving of Rajasthan

The forts and palaces and beautiful havelis of Rajasthan are all superb examples of the exquisite mason work of the state. Dholpur near Bharatpur and Barmer are popular for panels of frescoes for buildings, large statuaries, planters, and intricately carved elephants and horses as garden sculptures. White marble statues of deities are considered to be a specialty of Jaipur.

There are back lanes in Jaipur that ring with the sound of diamond-tipped chisels and hammers, carefully chipping away at blocks of marble and red or yellow sandstone. Till the royalty held sway in India, stone carving received ample patronage in the form of architectural commissions. In fact, when founding the city of Jaipur, Sawai Jai Singh earmarked a whole lane for stone carvers, naming it Silawaton ka Mohalla. Some of Jaipur's best showpieces are the latticework in the City Palace; the sandstone carvings and ornamental stonework at the Hawa Mahal and the Amber Fort gateways.

Today, the stone carvers have to make do with idol making and sculptures. The heart of this industry lies in the southwest quarter of Jaipur. White Makrana marble is carted here in roughly-shaped blocks. A row of holes is drilled and iron wedges hammered into it till the block breaks down along its line of weakness. To craft the figure, a vertical line is drawn along the axis and the sculptor keeps shaping the outline as he goes along. It's all done very carefully as even a slight crack renders the idol useless for worship. These men who transform stone into poetry, also fashion animals, human figures and plain geometric forms apart from gods and goddesses.

ARCHITECTURE OF RAJASTHAN

Nagda temple

Mâru-Gurjara architecture (*Rajasthani architecture*) originated in the sixth century in and around areas of the state of Rajasthan in India during Gurjara Pratihara Empire.

Etymology

The name *Maru Gurjara* has its genesis in the fact that during ancient times, Rajasthan and gujrat had similarities in ethentic, cultural and political aspects of the society. Ancient name of Rajasthan was *Marudesh* while Gujarat was called *Gurjaratra.*

"Maru Gurjara art" literally means "art of Rajasthan".

Development

Carved elephants on the walls of Jagdish Temple that was built by Maharana Jagat Singh Ist in 1651 A.D

Mâru-Gurjara Architecture show the deep understanding of structures and refined skills of Rajasthani craftmen of bygone era. *Mâru-Gurjara Architecture* has two prominent styles *Maha-Maru* and *Maru-Gurjara.* According to *M. A. Dhaky, Maha-Maru*style developed primarily in *Marudesa, Sapadalaksha,*

Surasena and parts of *Uparamala* whereas *Maru-Gurjara* originated in Medapata, Gurjaradesa-Arbuda, Gurjaradesa-Anarta and some areas of Gujarat. Scholars such as George Michell, M.A. Dhaky, Michael W. Meister and U.S. Moorti believe that *Mâru-Gurjara Temple Architecture* is entirely *Western Indian*architecture and is quite different from the North Indian Temple architecture. There is a connecting link between *Mâru-Gurjara Architecture* and Hoysala Temple Architecture. In both of these styles architecture is treated sculpturally.

Styles of Rajasthani architecture include:

- Jharokha
- Chhatri
- Haveli
- Stepwell (baoli or bawdi)
- Johad
- Jaali

Architecture in Rajasthan represents many different types of buildings, which may broadly be classed either as secular or religious. The secular buildings are of various scales. They include towns, villages, wells, gardens, houses, and palaces. All these kinds of buildings were meant for public and civic purposes. The forts are also included in secular buildings, though they were also used for defense and military purposes. The typology of the buildings of religious nature consists of three different kinds: temples, mosques, and tombs. The typology of the buildings of secular nature is more varied.

RAJASTHAN: ARCHITECTURE

Rajasthan state is certainly the most colorful state in the country. Rajasthan has an exclusive architecture and is well-known for its architecture all over the nation. Rajasthan's architecture is chiefly based on Rajput school of architecture which was an assortment of the Mughal and the Hindu structural plan.

The astonishing forts, the beautifully engraved temples and

the splendid Havelis of the Rajasthan state are essential parts of Rajasthan's architectural heritage. The Rajputs were productive designers and builders. Some impressive and splendid palaces and forts in the world mark the parched Aravalli milieu and tell the anecdotes of their magnificent bequest. The assortment and vividness of the architectural heritage of Rajasthan can stun a sightseer.

Some of the famous formations that symbolize the architectural legacy of Rajasthan areDilwara Temples, Chittaurgarh Fort, Lake Palace Hotel, Jaisalmer Havelis and City Palace.

Some styles of the architecture of Rajasthan include:

- Chhatri
- Jharokha
- Stepwell
- Haveli
- Johad

Styles Of Architecture

Chhatris are eminent, dome shaped porches used as a constituent in the architecture of India. The Chhatris are normally used to portray the fundamentals of admiration and pride in Rajasthan's Rajput architecture. They are extensively used, in forts, in palaces or to distinguish funerary locations. Instigating in the architecture of Rajasthan where there were memorials for royalty and kings, they were later on tailored as a typical characteristic in all constructions of Rajasthan, and most significantly in the Mughalarchitecture. They are at present seen in the premium shrines, Delhi's Humayun's Tomband Agra's Taj Mahal. In Hindi, the term "Chhatri" refers to a canopy or an umbrella.

A Jharokha is a kind of suspended enclosed gallery used in the architecture of India, characteristically in Rajasthani architecture, Mughal architecture and Rajputanaarchitecture. One of the most significant purposes it served was to permit women in Pardah to witness the events without being noticed themselves. On the other hand, these casements could also be used to place spies and archers.

Haveli is the idiom used for a private manor in Pakistan and India, typically one with architectural and historical implication. Haveli word is derived from the word Hawli which means an "enclosed place". Hawli is a Persian word. They share alike traits with other mansions derived from the Architecture of Islam such as the customary houses in Morocco that are called the Riads. Many Havelis in Pakistan and India were swayed by Central Asian, Indian architecture and Islamic Persian.

Stepwells are known by many names such as Kalyani, Pushkarani, Bawdi, Baoli, Baravor Vaav. These Stepwells are ponds or wells in which water can reach by sliding some steps. The Stepwells may be roofed and secluded and are frequently of architectural implication. The Stepwells are most widespread in the Western region of India.

A Johad is storage of rainwater in a tank mainly used in Rajasthan. It stores and collects water all through the year that is used for drinking by cattle and humans. In many areas of Rajasthan the yearly rainfall is very little thus; the water can be unlikable to drink. Rainfall during the months of July and August is stocked up in Johads and is used all through the year. Johads are called "Khadins" in Jaisalmer.

Temples Of Rajasthan

The immense architectural association which flounced Rajasthan from centuries was actually later blossoming of the virile expansion enthused by the Guptas. The Temples constructed around this instance also comprises of temples at Chittorgarh as well as Osiyan in the western part of Rajasthan. The recognizable characteristic of these temples are spire as well as intricately engraved external chamber known as the Mandap, earlier than the internal sanctum. Fine illustrations of some of the magnificent temples are the Kumbha Shyam temples and Kalika Mata Temple in Chittorgarh fortress.

Brahma Temple, Pushkar

Pushkar place is greatly acknowledged for the Brahma temple, although there are a lot many temples in Pushkar, with around 400 temples facing the banks of the lake. In the month of November, during the occasion of the yearly fair, Pushkar is a multihued gathering of people and revelry corresponding with the prime camel fair held in the planet.

Eklingji Temple, Udaipur

The originator of the Mewar Empire had an astounding vision in which he pleaded before a figure of Shiva which resulted in the elimination of his trouble that had been disturbing him in his daily life. He thought to construct a temple, and so the compound had its origin, 24 kilometers North of Udaipur. Eklingji temple consists of a compound of 108 temples, corresponding with the amount of beads in the necklace of Rudraksh that saints use for meditation.

Govind Devji Temple, Jaipur

The temple was sanctified as division of the City palace compound by Sawai Jai Singh. A holy place, with an untied marquee bounded by columns, and with a courtyard, curtsy and sacrament reverence at the shrine is considered lofty on the level of merit. Escalated on a gray throne, and festooned with gold jewelery, the statues are predominantly adored during Janamashtmi festival.

Shrinathji Temple, Nathdwara

A temple is dedicated to Lord Krishna with an illustration imprinted from a solitary chunk of black marble. At the holy place, hints of the deity are allowable for little periods at preset epochs of the daytime, and it is assumed that the faithful observe him in diverse moods allied with his life.

Dilwara Temple, Mt Abu

For many sightseers, this is the reason sufficient to stopover

Mt Abu. Situated inside a prehistoric mango orchard, the Dilwara temples are copiously imprinted and are unwrapped amid noon and 6 in the dusk. During the dawn, the clerics execute numerous sacrament rituals that are not open for the public.

Parsvanath Temple, Nakoda

The temple is located in a vale looped by hills, on the highway of Jodhpur-Barmer, the holy place devoted to the Tirthankara Parsvanath is engraved in black marble. Alongside it are some supplementary Jain temples, including the Shantinath temple.

Shri Mahavirji Temple

Positioned 90 kilometers from Ranthambhor area, it is assumed that the site was rehabilitated into a pilgrimage destination subsequent to the detection of an effigy of Mahavira by the cowherd. The Shri Mahavirji temple is a gigantic compound that has been erected with white stonework and has cupolas made of red stone.

Rishabdo Temple, Dhulev

A Rishabdo Temple compound that is delightfully carved, 64 kilometers from the Udaipur city, it is devoted to Rishabdeo, while descriptions of numerous other Tirthankaras are imprinted into panes on the fortifications.

Famous Stambs Of Rajasthan

Vijay Stambh

Vijay Stambh is also recognized as the 'Tower of Victory'. The Vijay Stambh was constructed by Rana Kumbha in 1440 A.D. It was built to mark the triumph over Malwa's Mahmud khilji. This commendable segment of architecture stands on a plinth at 10 feet towering and is assumed to have taken over ten years to be concluded. The 157 spherical and tapered steps which escorts to the patio is also a visible facet of the architecture.

Tazia Tower

Placed among the Jaisalmer's golden sand dunes of the

lavishness, the generous impression of tower is enhanced by the pleasant sites. Serving the residence of the prior regal folks, the creation is captivating with its shades of brilliance customarily parting the spectators enthralled. The marvelous 5 tiered construction rises from the Badal Mahal with every storey polished by a dexterously carved gallery.

Kirti Stambh

Kirti Stambh is a twenty-two meters elevated 7 storied tower constructed by a Jain merchant, Jijaji Kathod in Twelfth century. Entirely controlled in the Solanki architectural technique internal to Chittorgarh fortress, it is thirty feet at the pedestal and tapered down to fifteen feet at the summit with a confined staircase of 54 steps.

FAIRS

Pushkar Fair: The Kartik fair at Pushkar, mainly a bathing fair in the lake regarded as the holiest of holies by the Hindus is the biggest of all fairs. It attracts more than one lakh people. Pushkar is among the five main places of pilgrimage mentioned in the Hindu scriptures. It has a large number of temples including one of the two temples dedicated to Brahma in India.

According to mythology, the area where Pushkar now stands was once terrorised by a demon, Vijra Nabh, who murdered Brahma's children. On hearing this, the god appeared and killed the demon with a lotus flower. The petals of the flower fell at three places where three lakes including the Pushkar lake were formed. A dip in the lake is intended to ensure entry into heaven after death.

At the same time as the Kartik fair a cattle fair is also held at Pushkar. A large number of bards and minstrels are present to sing and recite ballads and traditional tales of valour and chivalry. The Pushkar fair is an attractive and lively spectacle with its colourful crowds, saffron-robed and ash smeared Sadhus and thousands of bulls, cows, sheep, goats and camels in richly decorated saddles.

The Kaila Devi Fair: The Kaila Devi Fair is one of the principal fairs of Rajasthan which is held from Chaitr Krishna 12 to Chaitr Shukla 12 at Kaila in the Karauli sub-division of Sawai Madhopur district.

The village was named Kalia after a sadhu called Kedar Giri who lived on the banks of the river Kali Sil. The images of Lakshmi and Chammunda can be seen in the temple of Kalia Mata. During the Yadavas rule, Maharaja Gopal Singh built a big temple with dome and a golden pinnacle. Number of buildings were constructed during the time of Maharaja Bhanwarpal and the area acquired vast popularity for its sanctity and scenic charm. The fair is held for a fortnight, during which animals are sacrificed outside the temple to propitiate the goddess. Traders from surrounding areas come to the fair and do brisk business. Rajputs, Meenas and members of the some other scheduled castes are among the principal devotees of Kaila Devi.

Sheetla Mata Fair: The Sheetla Mata Fair in honour of the goddess of small-pox is held in all village and towns on Sheetla Ashtama day.

The biggest fair is held in March-April every year at Seel-Ki-Doongri, a village in Jaipur district. There is a shrine dedicated to the Mata on a hillock, locally called Doongri. The present temple is said to have been erected by Maharaja Madho Singh of Jaipur. The fair is attended by one lakh or more people.

Sheetla Mata is among the Puranic goddess and venerated all over the country. She is addressed differently in different areas. In U. P she is known as Mata or Maha Mai, in western India as Mai Anama and in Rajasthan as Sadh, Sheetla or Sedal Mata. The word 'Sheetla' comes from sheetal. The belief is that Sheetla Mata appears in the form of small pox to calm the sufferer after he had been afflicted with high fever. This fair is also known as a fair of bullock-carts. The devotees of the Mata come from far and near in their decorated bullock-carts and the tinkling of bells tied to the necks of bullocks fills the air. The assemblage of these carts and their colourful occupants at the foot of the hillock crowned by the shrine is one of the memorable sights of Rajasthan.

Karni Mata Fair: The shrine of Karni Mata at Deshnok in the Nokha tehsil of Bikaner district is the venue of a fair twice a year. Both these fairs are held in Navaratra, the first in March-April and the second, which is smaller, in September-October. Deshnok is said to have been founded by Karni Mata in 1419.

There is a legend behind the Karni Mata Fair. Karni Bai was a strange girl with mysterious power. As she was the sixth girl in the family, her aunt wanted to cause her harm but the woman's arm was dislocated. At the age of five, Karni Bai cured her aunt's arm and her father who was bitten by a snake. She helped people with her supernatural powers.

On her way to Sind to meet her sister, Karni Bai met a blind carpenter at Jaisalmer. She asked him to make a wooden statue of her and rest his head on it when he lay down to sleep. The carpenter did so and found himself transported to Deshnok the next morning, where his sight was restored. Karni Mata is said to have died in 1538 and she has been worshipped as a goddess since then.

The temple of Karni Mata contains a 75 cm image of the deity. It is built of the yellow marble found in Jaisalmer. There is a mukat or crown on the head of the image and Karni Mata is shown weaning earnings. The temple of Karni Mata has been described as the temple of nice who roam freely about the shrine, unconcerned by the devotees who throng there. If anybody reads on a mouse and kills it, in repentance he has to present a silver mouse at the temple.

Kapil Muni Fair: The Kapil Muni fair is held every year on Kartik Purnima in Kolayat which is a sacred place near Bikaner. The word 'Kolayat' is derived from the Sanskrit word Kapilyatan.

Kolayat is located on a plateau which is part of Thar desert. Here a deep depression forms a lake where water is sweet and pure. The lake has fifty-two ghats. A statue of Kapil Muni has been installed at the main ghat.

According to the Skanda Purana, who was married to the daughter of Maharshi Manu. Kapil Muni attained the highest religious merit in boyhood and taught his mother the Sankhya Sastra. On his retirement to the Himalayas Kapil Muni came across on oasis and was bewitched by its beautiful surroundings. A part of his soul lingered there and oasis became famous and many devotees thronged it.

But the gods became jealous and hid it in the sandy desert. Skandh Deo, the son of Siva and Parvathi, took pity on suffering humanity and brought the place back to light. Great significance is attached to a dip in the holy lake which is supposed to Purge the devout of his sins.

There are many legends connected with the area, which tell of rebirths and vows made and broken and of rishis and munis who faltered and were saved. Through the centuries a number of miracles are said to have been performed due to the intercession of Kapil Muni. This belief still lingers to keep the fair going.

Banganga Fair: The Banganga Fair is held near a rivulet about 11km from Bairat, a historical township in Jaipur district. People come on the full moon day of Vaisakh to have a dip in the sacred stream which is supposed to have originated from the sport where Arjun shot an arrow.

The fair ground is surrounded by low hills and has an abundance of palm trees. The origin of the fair is shrouded in mystery. The fair started about 200 years ago, when the Radha-Krishna temple was erected. No feasts are held in the temple and the pilgrims bring their own food. The banks of the Banganga are studded with temples. Besides the Radha-Krishna temple, and by the side of the Nand Kund, is the shrine of Hanuman. Maharaja Ram Singh built the Har-Ki-Pauri. People gather at the temple a day before the fair starts and sing bhajans at night.

The Radha-Krishna temple is an impressive double storey

building. After ten steps, there is a shrine of Garuda facing the main idols of Krishna and Radha. On the four sides are Verandahs. One of them has the images of the Pandavas and their wife, Draupadi. In the right verandah is a row of lingas on which water flows through a common channel. One of the lingas has five faces carved on it. This is known as the Panch-Mikhi-Madhaeva of Ekdash Rudra.

Jambheswar Fair: The Jambheswar fair is in honour of Jambheswari who is the founder of the Bishnoi sect. Every year two fairs are held in his honour on Phalgun Budi Amavasya and Ashivan Budi Amavasya in Mukm village in Bikaner district. Phalgun Budi Amavasya is the biggest fair.

The Bishnois form a separate sect and do not mix with other Hindus and worship Vishnu in his Jambhaji incarnation. The Bishnois believe that the city of Viskramaditya, with its throne of gold, is buried beneath the sand dune where the saint died. Jambheshwarji was the thirty-second descendant of Vikramaditya. According to legend, he was found under a tree and tended cows till the age of twelve. He is supposed to have been dumb in childhood but wrought a self-miracle which gave him speech. He later gave up the occupation of cowherd and settled down on the top of a hill where he gave the Bishnois the twenty-nine articles of their religion. The word 'Bisnoi' is a combination of 'bees' (twenty) and 'noi' (nine)- The followers of the twenty-nine articles of faith laid down by Jambeshwarji.

Sitabari Fair: Sitabari is a small place near Kelwara village in the Sahabad tehsil of Kota district and the fair is held from Baisakh Sudi Punam to Jeth Budi Amavasya. Sitabari is situated in a picturesque forest. According to legend, it marks the spot where Sita was left by Lakshman at the behest of Rama. There are four tanks filled by natural springs. The water is said to cure people of various ailments, particularly mental diseases. The water in these Kunda is cold in summer and warm in winter and the kunds never go dry. The Sitabari fair attracts thousands people who take a bath in the Sita Kund, the Laxman Kund and the Suraj Kund-which are regarded as holy as the Ganges.

Priesthood at the shrine is hereditary and there are various priests attached to the kunds. No offerings are made at the fourth kund which is knows as Bharat Kund because it is considered inauspicious to do so.

Urs of Khwaja Moinuddin Chishti: Urs of Khawaja Moinuddin Chishti at Ajmer is the biggest attraction for the Muslims. Over two lakh Muslims assemble here to pay homage to the memory of the saint at his dargah (mausoleum). The localities around the dargah present gay spectacle on this occasion. Many devotees arrange feasts, known as Niyaz for the poor. Rich among the devotees arrange qawwalis and recitations of Milad Sharif. During the qawwalis, many spectators go into trance, quivering and moving their bodies briskly, repeating the refrain of the qawwalis along with qawwals. This state of trance is known as hal and often scores of people are affected by it.

Pilgrims make rich offerings at the holy spot where the Khwaja is entombed in the dargah. The Khwaja is believed to possess miraculous powers and can ensure the birth of a son, cure ailments, ward off evil spirits and bring good luck. From the architectural point of view the dargah is unique.

Galiyakot Urs: The Urs at Galiyakot attracts Davoodi Bohras from all over the country. Galiyakot is a small village situated on the banks of the Mahi river in the interior of the Sagwara tehsil of picturesque Dungarpur district. It is the place where Syedi Fahruddin, the venerated saint of the Bohras lies buried.

The shrine of the saint is near the village. The mausoleum has a beautiful dome sixteen metres highs and six metres wide. There is a mosque by the side of the shrine where women can offer prayers. There are a number of graves around the dargah and in one of them lies buried Bhai Sahib, the son of the saint. The Son of Tarmal, Syedi, Fakrhuddin in his wanderings came to the village of Galiyakot where he died and was buried. He performed many miracles, and pilgrims from India and abroad visit the shrine to seek his intercession. His Urs is celebrated on the twenty seventh of Moharrum, according to the Egyptian calendar which differs from the Hijri Calendar followed by Sunni Muslims.

Jeen Mata and Annakoot Fairs: Jeen Mata fair is held at the shrine of Jeen Mata, a few kilometers from Goriyan railway station in Sikar district, during the Navaratras. Rajputs and Meenas, who worship Kali as the principal deity, throng this shrine and make offering of wine and meat obtained by sacrificing goats and buffalos. The Meenas lend colour and music to the scene.

Jeen Mata occupies an important place amongst the local deities of Rajasthan. There is a saying in Rajasthan that those who have not had a 'darshan' of the Jeen Mata temple, have not seen anything.

There are many stories about the deity and miracles performed by Jeen. Jeen Mata temple is located in Adabla Girmala village, south of Rivasi in Sikar district. A mela is held on the occasion of Durga Puja in the temple every year. There is an eight-faced statue of the Devi. Two lamps are lit in front of the statue all the time. It is said that wishes of worshippers are fulfilled after 'darshan' of Jeen Mata.

The Annakoot fair is held in Udaipur district at Nathdwara which is the principal set of the Ballabh sect of Vaishnavas. On Annakoot day, a mountain of food is erected to satisfy the hunger of the lord of the universe. A huge pile of baked rice is prepared in the courtyard of this famous shrine which is grabbed by the Bhils as the Prasad of Kalia Baba. As soon as the doors of the shrine are throngs open, throngs of singing and dancing Bhils rush into the temple and clear up this pile. They keep the rice as a medicine, for they believe it cures many ailments. Parcels of this sacred gift are sent to friends and relatives.

Adivasi Fairs: The most important of the Adivasi fairs is held at Baneshwar in the Aspur tehsil of Dungarpur district in southern Rajasthan. The site of the fair is a small delta formed by the confluence of the river Som with the Mahi. One has to wade to the fair through the Som. The word 'Baneshwar' is derived from the Siva Linga of the area. A delta is known as 'van' in Wagad (sparsely populated area). This Vaneshwar or Baneshwar means the Master of the Delta.

The linga in the area is said to be self-born. It is small and its top is broken into five parts. The present temple was built by Maharawal Askaran of Dungarpur. Near the temple of Baneshwar there is the temple of Vishnu built by Jankunwari, the daughter-in-law of Mavji, a highly revered saint of the area, who was supposed to be an incarnation of Vishnu. Mavji is said to have written five books called 'Chopras'. The original book is read every year at Diwali by the Goswami (priest) of the temple. Mavjis equestrain temple is the main idol of worship. After Mavji, his son succeeded him. Two disciples of Mavji built the third temple in the area which is called as the Laskshmi-Narain temple.

The tribal fair is held from Magh Shukla Ekadashi to Magh Shukla Purnima (Feb.- Mar). Only the priest is permitted to touch the idols. Most of the devotees are Bhils and every night they sing round a bonfire.

Hero-worship Fairs: Hero worship has been a tradition among the Rajasthanis and important fairs are held in honour and veneration of their heroes. At the fairs held in honour of Ramdeoji, Gogaji and Tejaji the people's deep spirituality as well as their life and culture manifest themselves.

Ramdeoji Fair: Ramdeora fair is held every year for ten days in August-September to pay homage to the fifteenth century saint, Shri Ramdeoji. Ramdeora village lies about 13 km from Pokaran, headquarters of a sub-division in Jaisalmer district.

Ramdeoji was a Tomar Rajput. Hindus regard him as an incarnation of Lord Krishna, while Muslims venerate him as Ramshah Pir. There is a story behind the birth of Ramdeoji. In the twelfth century, King Anangpal decided to go on a pilgrimage and as he had no son, he entrusted the administration of his kingdom to Pritviraj Chauhan, his maternal grandson. Prithviraj refused to restore the kingdom to King Anangpal, who had returned from the pilgrimage and the King and his descendant settled in the part of Jaisalimer which is known as Shiv tehsil.

One of Anangpal's descendants Ajmall, was a great devotee of Dwarkadhesh (Lord Krishna). Because of his devotion Dwarkadhesh decided to take birth as his son. The child was named Ramdeo. Ramdeo soon became famous as a saintly man and five pirs from Mecca came to test him, and they were impressed by Ramdeo and paid him obeisance.

Ramdeoji is considered a saint who devoted his life to the uplift of the downtrodden. He buried himself alive. Around Ramdeoji's grave a magnificent temple was built by Maharaja Ganga Singh of Bikaner. Wooden toy horses covered with cloth are among the most popular offerings at the temple. It is one of the famous fairs in Rajasthan.

Veerpuri Fair: The Veerpuri fair is held at Mandor to commemorate the heroes of Rajasthan. The site is about 10km from Jodhpur. The fair is held on the penultimate Monday of Shravan. There are two legends about its origin.

According to one, Jaswant Singh who ruled Mandor was sent to Ahmednagar by Aurangzeb to crush a rebellion. Jaswant Singh prayed to old heroes of his land for success and was able to win the battle. He built a gallery of heroes at Mandor and every year on the last Monday of Shravan he visited to pay respect to the heroes.

The second legend concerning the origin of the fair relates to Veerpuja. During Mughal days, a Rajput youth had to leave his unmarried sister alone to join a battle. The sister applied tilak to her brothers forehead and he returned victorious from battle.

Rani Sati Fair: Rani Sati fair was held in Jhunjhunu town twice a year, on Magh-Krishna Navami and Bhadrapada Amavasya. It was on Magh Krishna Navami that Rani Sati, the first of the series of thirteen Satis of the Jalan family, immolated herself. The last Sati was on Bhadrapada Amavasya. As Rani was the first Sati in her family, the fair is held in her name.

There was a legend behind the fair. The Jali Ram, the diwan of Nawab of Hissar had a son Tandhan Ram who owned a fine mare. The son of Nawab of Hissar wanted the mare for himself. When his request was refused, he decided the steal the horse. Tandhan Ram threw his spear at the thief and killed him. Nawab of Hissar attacked Tandham Ram and killed him while he was returning with his wife Narainidevi to Jhunjhunu. Narainidevi took away the body of her husband and immolated herself on the funeral pyre and later appeared as a goddess. Her principal followers are Jalans, who are the descendants of another son of Jali Ram.

Mallinath Fair: The Mallinath fair held annually for a fortnight during March-April in the dry bed of the river Luni near Tilwara in Barmer is one of the biggest fairs in Rajasthan. Camels, horses, goats and sheep are brought and sold at the fair. An image of Mallinath has been installed in the temple where offerings of batashas and laddoos are made during the fair. Replicas of horses are also offered as a mark of respect.

Gogaji Fair: Gogaji fair is held in Gogamedi village in Ganganagar district in honour of Gogaji. The fair is held from the ninth day of the dark half of Bhadrapada (Goga Navami) to the eleventh day of the dark half of the same month. Gogaji Samadhi is made of white marble. His idol depicts him with a spear in hand riding a horse. His whip is also worshipped and he is supposed to be a patron of barren women. Replicas of his horse are worshipped on Goga Navami.

FESTIVALS OF RAJASTHAN

When we think about Rajasthan, we think of colors and brightness, royalty and hospitality, celebrations and feasts, music and dance, culture and tradition, history and heritage.

Rajasthan packs the essence of Incredible India in 1 state. And the experience of Rajasthan is never complete unless you have a taste of the myriad fairs and festivals that it has to offer. They are a celebration of life, culture, heritage, and nature, in true *Rajasthani* style. Here are some of the festivals of Rajasthan you must experience at least once in your lifetime

Rajasthan International Folk Festival, Jodhpur

Platform for Creativity and Sustainable Development? and patronised by the Maharaja of Jodhpur and Sir Mick Jagger of the Rolling Stones, RIFF is an annual music and art festival for the promotion of traditional folk music and arts. It is celebrated around Sharad Purnima, the brightest full moon night of the year and is a unique celebration of Indian as well as international music at Jodhpur?s Mehrangarh fort. More than 200 musicians from around the globe attend this festival, making it an absolute treat for music and art lovers. It coincides with the Marwar festival.

Desert Festival, Jaisalmer

A three-day event organised by the Rajasthan Tourism Development Corporation in the month of February, it is an absolute bonanza that celebrates the delights of the desert. The atmosphere is alive with song and dance, with the artists dressed in bright colours and traditional finery, depicting the tragedies and accomplishments of the desert. A showcase of desert rituals and life, camel races, gymnastic stunts, several competitions like longest moustache, turban tying, Mr Desert etc, delicious food and interesting stalls selling handicrafts and other souvenirs will make it a memorable 3 days of your life.

Pushkar Fair, Pushkar

The Big Daddy of all desert festivals, Pushkar Fair is a spectacular five-day camel and livestock fair held in the town of Pushkar, on the banks of the Pushkar lake in Rajasthan. It also coincides with the religious celebration of Kartik Ekadashi, when the Pushkar lake was supposed to be created by Lord Brahma. Primarily a livestock fair for the buying and selling of camels, the Pushkar fair attracts hordes of tourists making it a true cultural bonanza of art, music, dance, puppet shows, gypsy dance, races, competitions with a host of vendors selling delicious snacks including camel milk cheeses and cakes, jewellery, shawls and other titbits. The entire festive and spiritual atmosphere completely lights up the desert in these five days.

Teej Festival, Jaipur

One of west India?s biggest festivals, Teej commemorates two things ? a woman?s love for her husband and the advent of the monsoon season. The festival is marked by colourful celebrations where the womenfolk observe fasting and apply mehndi designs on their hands, enjoy long swing rides, song and dance with other women, tell stories and deck up in festive attire to celebrate the union of Lord Shiva and Goddess Parvati. The markets and bazaars of Jaipur are filled to the brim with attractive clothes, jewellery and sweets like *Ghewar* and *Malpua*. A procession of a decorated idol of Goddess Parvati is carried through Jaipur, and thousands of devotees and tourists throng to see the procession and the antique palanquins, chariots, bands, folk music and dance and soak in the cultural revelry.

Gangaur Festival, Jaipur

Another festival that commemorates the goddess Parvati and

her home-coming, it is celebrated with huge fanfare in Rajasthan by women. Processions of a decked up Goddess Gauri are carried all over the city and everyone participates in these processions, often accompanied by elephant processions, old palanquins, chariots, folk song and dance and often ends with fireworks. It coincides with the Mewar festival in Udaipur.

Jaipur Literature Festival, Jaipur

Perhaps not as glamorous as some of the other festivals on this list, JLF is the world?s largest free literary festival. Nobel laureates, Booker prize winners, debut novelists ? the who?s who of the literary world come together for five days of readings, discussions and debates at the Diggi Palace in Jaipur. A great platform that provides access to some of the greatest authors and thinkers on this planet and gives courage to young minds to dream and imagine, it is not a chance anyone should miss.

Nagaur Fair, Nagaur

The second largest fair in the country, it is essentially a cattle fair that attracts more than two lakh animal owners to bring their horses, cows, bullocks, oxen, camels etc. to be a part of a large trade show. A lot of animal races and cockfights in the day, followed by some dance and music in the nights attracts tourists and animal owners alike. Organised by the Department of Animal Husbandry, it brings out the true Rajput flavour of Rajasthan.

Summer and Winter Festivals, Mt. Abu

Celebrated to showcase the warmth and culture of the people belonging to the only hill station in Rajasthan, both these festivals are held over a period of three days, in May and December respectively. They are marked by processions all over town, followed by a range of competitions, folk dance and music and dazzling fireworks to celebrate the spirit of the town. A unique combination of divine hospitality and exotic location attracts a large number of tourists during the festival days.

World Sufi Spirit Festival, Gangaur, Jodhpur

Hosting artists from Mongolia, Afghanistan, Africa, Italy etc. and also from various parts of the state and the country, it is a very exclusive event that attracts a limited number of patrons. A very simple affair means you can sit down to chat with some of the brilliant artists or even the royalty of Jodhpur. Add to that some delicious food and the ambience of the spectacularly lit-up Nagaur fort, and you will surely have the experience to cherish for a lifetime.

Kite Festival, Jodhpur

A 3-day festival to celebrate the spirit of Makar Sankranti, the Jodhpur International Desert Kite Festival, is simply put, a kite-flying competition. In reality, it is a colourful and extravagant spectre of kites, of myriad shapes, colours and sizes that deck up the desert sky. A number of helicopters release kites in the sky and children release balloons, making it a truly magnificent and spectacular event.

Camel Festival, Bikaner

Organised in the honour of the ship of the desert, the Camel Festival is a spectacular festival celebrated in Bikaner. Just like the other celebrations of Rajasthan, this festival kicks off with great pomp and show. Celebrated every year in the pleasant January, the Camel Festival is a two-day long affair with a colourful parade of the decked up camels against the backdrop of the magnificent Junagadh Fort.

It includes camel race, camel games and other cultural performances. Though celebrated to glorify the camels of Rajasthan, this festival also includes the traditional Rajasthani folk performances.

The festival concludes with an awe-inspiring display of fireworks, illuminating the majestic skies of Bikaner.

Mewar Festival, Udaipur

The city of Udaipur comes alive with colours of festivities

during the Mewar Festival which marks the advent of spring in the region. It is a major festival of Rajasthan and people from all over the globe flock to Udaipur to witness the glory of the town during this time. The whole town is decorated with bright lights and a joyous mood reigns in the air. This festival includes a number of practices, like dressing the idols of Isar and Gangaur and carrying them in a traditional procession through various parts of the city. People also engage in the cultural dance and songs, revealing the colourful culture of Rajasthan.

Urs Festival, Ajmer

Usually held in the month of May and June, the Urs Festival is one of the major festivals celebrated at the venerated Ajmer Sharif Dargah. Hordes of pilgrims travel to this town, located to the West of Jaipur to visit this holy shrine. The Urs Festival commemorates the death anniversary of Khwaja Moinuddin Chisti, the revered Sufi Saint. The fair is held for six days because it is believed that the Khwaja Moinuddin cooked for six days before he left his mortal remains. His followers from all over the world throng Ajmer to seek his blessings during these six sacred days.

Brij Holi, Bharatpur

The most loved festival in India is celebrated in a grand and elaborate style, a few days ahead before Holi, in Bharatpur located in the Brij region of Rajasthan. The spirit of the city comes alive during this festival, with people dressed in their brightest attires and singing colourful songs. Lord Krishna is worshipped in this festival, thus the entire love story of Krishna and Radha is showcased in the form of a dance, which is the unique feature of this festival. The entire region is immersed in the colours of Holi during this time and the people are at their merriest self. Tourists from far and wide come to Bharatpur to experience the out of the world festivities.

Kota Adventure Festival

Combine adventure with spirituality and you have the Kota Adventure Festival! It is one of the fascinating festivals of Rajasthan, held during Dussehra in the month of October. During this festival, adventure sports are organised which beckons people from every part of the country. The main aim of the festival is to boost the tourism of the state. It is a week-long haven for adventure enthusiasts since the key events include rafting, windsurfing, parasailing, kayaking rock climbing, trekking, angling and rural excursions. The main highlight of the festival is kite flying. Name any adventure sports and you would probably find it at the Kota Adventure Festival.

Elephant Festival, Jaipur

The hub of grand festivals and celebrations, Rajasthan, is the centre for the unique and much awaited Camel Festival, held annually in the Pink City, Jaipur. The festival is organised to highlight the importance of elephants in Rajasthan and takes place during the time of Holi. Groomed to perfection and glittering in gold, the elephants catwalk amidst an enthralled audience, with musicians playing the folk songs. Games like elephant polo, elephant race, tug-of-war, and elephant decoration are the highlights of this festival. It commemorates with the people mounting on the elephants and playing with colours. This unique festival is definitely a once-in-a-lifetime experience.

Chandrabhaga Fair, Jhalawar

Jhalawar is a princely state located in south-eastern Rajasthan which is the host to the Chandrabhaga Fair every year during the month of October and November. This is predominantly a cattle fair which is held on the auspicious day of Kartik Purnima when thousands of people take a dip in the holy Chandrabhaga River. It is considered a holy place by the local people who call is Chandravati. Just like the famous Pushkar fair, this fair also organises the cattle fair where livestock is available for re-sale. Traders and merchants from all over the country flock here and take part in this fair.

10

Education

During recent years, Rajasthan has worked on improving education. The state government has been making sustained efforts to raise the education standard.

Literacy

In recent decades, the literacy rate of Rajasthan has increased significantly. In 1991, the state's literacy rate was only 38.55% (54.99% male and 20.44% female). In 2001, the literacy rate increased to 60.41% (75.70% male and 43.85% female).

This was the highest leap in the percentage of literacy recorded in India (the rise in female literacy being 23%). At the Census 2011, Rajasthan had a literacy rate of 67.06% (80.51% male and 52.66% female). Although Rajasthan's literacy rate is below the national average of 74.04% and although its female literacy rate is the lowest in the country, the state has been praised for its efforts and achievements in raising literacy rates.

In rural areas of Rajasthan, the literacy rate is 76.16% for males and 45.8% for females. This has been debated across all the party level except BJP, when the governor of Rajasthan set a minimum educational qualification for the village panchayat elections.

Schools

Rajasthan has 55,000 primary and 7,400 secondary schools.

Higher education

In Rajasthan, Jodhpur and Kota are major education hubs. Kota is known for its quality education in preparation for competitive exams, coaching for medical and engineering exams, while Jodhpur is home to many higher education institutions like IIT, AIIMS, National Law University, Sardar Patel Police University, National Institute of Fashion Technology, MBM Engineering College etc. Kota is popularly referred to as, "coaching capital of India". Other major education institutions are Birla Institute of Technology and Science Pilani, Indian Institute of Technology Jodhpur, Indian Institute of Information Technology, Kota, Malaviya National Institute of Technology, Jaipur, IIM Udaipur, AIIMS Jodhpur and LNMIIT.

Rajasthan has nine universities and more than 250 colleges. There are 41 engineering colleges with an annual enrollment of about 11,500 students. Apart from above there are 41 private universities like Madhav University, Singhania University, Pacheri Bari Amity University Rajasthan (Jaipur), Mewar University Chittorgarh, OPJS University, Churu, Mody University of Technology and Science Lakshmangarh (Women's University, Sikar), RNB Global University, Bikaner. The state has 23 polytechnic colleges and 152 Industrial Training Institutes (ITIs) that impart vocational training.

In 2009, Central University of Rajasthan a central university fully funded by Government of India, came into force near Kishangarh in Ajmerdistrict.

RAJASTHAN VIDYAPEETH

History: Rajasthan Vidyapeeth (Deemed University) was founded by Pandit Janardan Rai Nagar in 1937 with the objective of uplifting the browbeaten common man in the feudalistic state of Mewar in Rajasthan. Originally it was established as a night education centre for the primary, secondary and advanced Courses in Hindi, the national language of the country and was named as Hindi Vidhyapeeth.

After the amalgamation of the state of Rajasthan, new dimensions were added and Hindi Vidhyapeeth was transformed into a prominent Non-Government Organization and hence was renamed as Rajasthan Vidyapeeth.

Present Status: The Evening College (Shramjeevi College) imparted education to those students, especially the underprivileged children who were engaged in work during the daytime and were keen in educating themselves in the evenings for better job prospects.

The Vidyapeeth also initiated a large number of other institutes like the Secondary School, Higher Secondary School, Post-basic School and the Centre for Fine Arts to impart education to all sections of the society. The College of Teachers' Training was another significant addition under the education system of Rajasthan Vidyapeeth in the seventies.

In 1987 the Rajasthan Vidyapeeth was granted the status of a deemed-to-be-University by the University Grants Commission and the Ministry of Human Resource Development, Government of India. Over the years, Rajasthan Vidyapeeth has developed into a large complex body with more than 50 institutions that is spread over many districts of the State. It now offers numerous courses and provides research -oriented qualitative education through preservation of socio-cultural values.

Administration: A unique feature of the administration of Rajasthan Vidyapeeth is based on democratic way of work and is termed as Janatantriaya Shilanyas (Democratic Foundation). The administration of Vidyapeeth is very organized and involves active participation of its workers in the decision making matters with the help of constituent bodies.

RAJASTHAN SANSKRIT UNIVERSITY, JAIPUR

Sanskrit has played a significant role in the linguistic background of India. Sanskrit has greatly helped in the development of the Indian languages and also in the conservation of the cultural heritage of the country. In fact Sanskrit is the language from which major Indian languages have evolved. Sanskrit also provided the theoretic foundation of ancient sciences. So it is very important to propagate and preserve the Sanskrit language for the Hence, it becomes essential to preserve and propagate Sanskrit for over all development of the country.

With this view the Rajasthan Sanskrit University or the Sanskrit Vishwavidalaya was set up in Jaipur for the development and preservation of the Sanskrit language and also to propagate and promote Sanskrit learning in the state.

The Rajasthan Sanskrit University in Jaipur offers research-oriented studies and programme offering the degree of Vidyavaridhi (Ph.D). The University also imparts education in subjects like Sahitya (Literature), Jyotish (Astrology), Vyakarana (Grammar) and Darshan (Philpsophy) at the Acharya level, Shastri level and Shiksha Shastri level. The Vice Chancellor of the University is Shri S N Thanvi while Shri G B Chaturvedi is the Registrar of Rajasthan Sanskrit University.

RAJASTHAN DENTAL COLLEGES

Dental Colleges are the institutions that run Dental and General hospitals that provide with Under Graduate and Post Graduate teaching facilities as approved by the Dental Council of India. At Present the state of Rajasthan has 9 Dental Colleges.

Three colleges are in the Public sector and the remaining six colleges are in the private sector.

These dental colleges produce expert professionals every year thus promoting Medical Tourism in the state.

Rajasthan Tourism already attracts a lot of domestic and foreign tourists.

These tourists are now enjoying expertise dental opinion as part of their vacation package due to reasonable dental cure programmes in the country.

RAJASTHAN EDUCATION INITIATIVE (REI)

Led by the Chief Minister of Rajasthan, Vasundhara Raje, the REI was launched at the India Economic Summit in November 2005 in New Delhi. Partners of the REI include the Government of Rajasthan, World Economic Forum, Confederation of Indian Industry (CII) and the Global Schools and Communities Initiative of the UNICT task force (GeSCI). The REI will play a facilitating role in the creation and implementation of public private partnerships through projects that focus on improving the delivery of educational services, and in particular on promoting equitable access, enrolment and retention of children in schools, reducing gender disparities, promoting skill development and enhancing learning levels.

Strategies

- Evolving innovative and locally appropriate models of PPPs with a high potential for being scaled up, for improving educational outcomes
- Adopting and adapting best practices from both the public and private sector while ensuring community participation
- Deploying new technologies, particularly ICTs, for modernizing educational service delivery, skill development and quality learning
- Enhancing the flow of resources into the educational sector in Rajasthan by structuring suitable projects and creating incentives for increased participation of different stakeholders.

The REI is an ambitious initiative aimed at balancing the goal of Education for all, through a two-pronged approach.

RAJASTHAN EDUCATION INITIATIVE PARTNERSHIP DESCRIPTION

The Rajasthan Education Initiative (REI) is a new venture aimed at engaging global and local partners from the private sector, foundations and NGOs in innovative multi-stakeholder partnerships to support education in the State of Rajasthan.

The Government of Rajasthan has created the REI with the support of the World Economic Forum, the Confederation of Indian Industry, and GeSCI - the Global e-Schools and Communities Initiative. Through this Partnership Document, the four "core partners" agree upon the vision and objectives for the Rajasthan Education Initiative, note some possible projects that could be supported or built upon through multi-stakeholder partnerships, and identify possible governance and management structures for the Initiative.

CONTEXT AND BACKGROUND

Rajasthan is the largest State in the Indian Union. With 10% of the landmass of the country and 5% of its population, it presents huge challenges in terms of development and socio-economic growth. Two-thirds of the State is desert with severe water shortages and other attendant disadvantages. The feudal history of the State combined with its natural geographical singularities, render Government developmental programmes difficult to implement, monitor and evaluate. Nevertheless, in the recent past, strenuous efforts have been made to lift the State above restraining factors. New oil finds in the State have also generated much optimism.

Given these natural disadvantages, the State fully realizes that the prospects of all-round development can be improved only if care is taken to develop available human resources. In the past, Rajasthan as a State has authored educational models that have ushered in sweeping changes through innovation and public participation. The now internationally acknowledged Shiksha Karmi Project and the Lok Jumbish Project helped to generate interest in education in far flung areas of the State by utilizing local talent and motivating children to attend schools.

The doubling of literacy rates in the State in the last decade is a clear indication of the impact that these measures have had on the population at large. Education in the State received new impetus with the World Bank assisted District Primary Education Projects in 19 Districts, and of course, the Sarva Shiksha Abhiyan (Education For All) since 2002. In the recent past, determined efforts have been made to provide access to schools for all children, to fill up vacancies of teachers and to provide free textbooks. The hot cooked mid-day meals programme for all primary school children has also ensured higher levels of enrolment and retention.

The State Government realizes that much ground still remains to be covered and that enlisting the support of all the relevant stakeholders including the private sector, civil society and other voluntary organizations in critical areas of education will yield results that can be effectively demonstrated and that can help inspire similar activities within the traditional education sector. This realization has led the State's government and its partners to think deeply and about how to optimise all available resources, and bring new resources to bear, to support achieving the desired goals.

The present Rajasthan Education Initiative arises from this thinking. Specifically, the REI emerged from discussions held by the Chief Minister of Rajasthan with business, political and NGO leaders in the World Economic Forum Annual Meeting held at Davos in January 2005. Based on the lessons learnt from the Jordan Education Initiative, Rajasthan has evolved for the REI its own definition of public-private partnership in the field of education, involving not only technological interventions in schools, but also socially relevant initiatives to help in the holistic development of the child.

The REI will have a unique position within the education sector positioning Rajasthan. Under the over arching vision of the Millennium Development Goals, and the specific thrust of the Sarva Shiksha Abhiyan, the REI will position itself as an outstanding example of public-private partnership which will have the energy and capacity to transform education and bring about a long-term beneficial impact on the development of the human resources of the State.

VISION STATEMENT

The Rajasthan Education Initiative will serve as an umbrella under which innovative multi stakeholder partnerships are catalysed by engaging the global and local private sector, foundations and charitable organisations and other grass roots level NGOs in support of Rajasthan's education objectives.

The main education objectives identified for Rajasthan by its Government are:

- Access - 100% enrolment in primary education by 2010, 100% enrolment in secondary education by 2020
- Retention - increase numbers finishing primary school to 100% by 2010 and for secondary to considerable higher levels.
- Girls' Education - increase access and retention of girls in primary to near 100% levels and in secondary to levels that will enable them lead productive lives with employment opportunities.
- Learning Achievement - increase quality of learning, especially in areas of Maths, Science and English.
- Empowering for a Global Knowledge Economy - expanding curriculum to provide ICT skills to secondary school students and to enable formation of human capital for the economy.

Objectives: The REI will focus on improving the delivery of educational services, and in particular on promoting equitable access, enrolment and retention of children in schools, reducing gender disparities, promoting skill development and enhancing learning levels. The REI will seek to bring a new educational paradigm to the State, based on the following strategies:

- Evolving innovative and locally appropriate models of PPPs with a high potential for being scaled up, for improving educational outcomes
- Adopting and adapting best practices from both the public and private sector while ensuring community participation
- Deploying new technologies, particularly ICTs, for modernizing educational service delivery, skill development and quality learning
- Creating systems for enabling greater community participation in the State's educational programme

- Enhancing the flow of resources into the educational sector in Rajasthan by structuring suitable projects and creating incentives for increased participation of different stakeholders
- Focus efforts on serving underprivileged communities in urban and rural areas as well as on the girl children and children with special needs
- Demonstrating the success of such public-private partnership interventions, by evaluating its impact on students with reference to the overall objectives of the Sarva Shiksha Abhiyan
- Disseminating the outcomes and learnings from the REI for replication in other parts of the State, other states in India as well as in other developing countries

The overall objective of the REI will be to demonstrate robust, sustainable and scalable models, approaches, tools and methodologies that can significantly impact educational outcomes and transform the educational scenario of the State.

ROLES OF THE CORE PARTNERS

The State Government and the three other core partners, namely, the World Economic Forum, the Global e-Schools and Communities Initiative and the Confederation of Indian Industries are committed to the achievement of the objectives of the Initiative and determined to work together for demonstrating the success of this public-partnership model in the field of the Education in the State.

These three core partners will facilitate and assist the State Government in the implementation, monitoring and reporting of the individual projects within the REI and evaluate the success of each of them so as to learn lessons from the experience. Efforts shall also be undertaken to encourage the participation of more stakeholders willing to take part in this model of public-private partnership.

The core partners will also assist the State Government of Rajasthan to explore the possibilities for scaling up the individual pilot projects presently under execution once their success has been demonstrated, so that a wider canvas with a greater number of schools and students can be benefited with the power of ICT intervention in education and the other related projects involving social responsibility programmes. It is our joint endeavour to work together to transform education in Rajasthan. Government of Rajasthan:

As leader and driver of the Rajasthan Education Initiative, the Government of the State shall:

1. Drive the programme and bring substantial public funding into REI
2. Ensure that efforts within the REI are aligned with broader objectives of the State and ensure smooth collaboration in such efforts
3. Undertake efforts to scale up successful PPPs catalysed under the REI and to bring them within the SSA and other government supported programmes.

Confederation of Indian Industry: The Confederation of Indian Industry (CII) works to create and sustain an environment conducive to the growth of industry in India, partnering industry and government alike through advisory and consultative processes. It is a non-government, not-for-profit organization which endeavours to catalyse change by working with government on policy issues, while providing a platform for sectoral consensus building and networking. CII will:

Endeavour to garner resources and skills for the REI in mobilizing its membership especially amongst Rajasthan's small and medium scale enterprises ensuring the creation of local capabilities and capacities in making the REI sustainable.

GeSCI—the Global e-Schools and Communities Initiative: The Global e-Schools and Communities Initiative (GeSCI), founded by the UN ICT Task Force, has the mission to improve education, empower communities and accelerate socio-economic development, this supporting the achievement of the Millennium

Development Goals through the wide-spread deployment of ICT in schools. Its approach is to catalyse, support and collaborate with national/regional initiatives in the design and implementation of end-to-end systems for attaining desired educational objectives and developmental goals. GeSCI will support the REI in several ways:

1. Facilitate the strategic planning and implementation for REI and assist the Government of Rajasthan in structuring the Initiative for ensuring optimal value.
2. Support the setting up of the REI project management office.
3. Provide access to the services of its own specialist personnel and other experts from partner organisations of GeSCI, in key areas such as technology options, content and monitoring & evaluation.
4. Leverage its knowledge capabilities and its network of global partners to ensure that international best practices are applied in the REI.
5. Deploy a full-time Facilitator in Rajasthan to deliver or enable delivery of the above services, and provide advice and support to the Government of Rajasthan on the REI and on ICTs in Education generally.

World Economic Forum: The World Economic Forum is an independent international organisation committed to improving the state of the world by engaging leaders in partnerships to shape the global, regional and industry agenda. It is a non-for-profit foundation and is tied to no political, partisan or national interests. The World Economic Forum will bring its unique capabilities in catalyzing private public partnerships by engaging its global membership and providing expert support in the management of PPPs Common Roles:

Together, the core partners will utilize their particular talents and core competencies to engage the private sector in the REI and synergise corporate and other energies into the specific projects identified for implementation as well as for new projects.

Furthermore, they will take common responsibility for the overall oversight and evaluation of the Initiative, through governance structures along lines such as those outlined below.

POSSIBLE AREAS FOR PUBLIC-PRIVATE PARTNERSHIPS

The REI envisages an integrated strategy revolving around two work-streams:

- Using technological interventions for effective delivery of educational instructions; and
- Creating an enabling environment in which effective learning can take place, including care and concern of disadvantaged students.

In these two areas, the following ongoing initiatives have been identified.

New Technology Interventions: The following ICT interventions are in the process of implementation in the State:

- *Project GRACE (Girls of Rajasthan and Computer Education):* Under the ICT Schools programme of the Government of India for 100 senior secondary girls' schools of educationally backward blocks of the State. Partnerships can be evolved for support especially for connectivity and power in remote areas and maintenance.
- *District Computer Training Centres:*In each of the 32 District headquarters where about 30-40 computers are available.

  Support can be invited for developing sustainable business models for funding these centres and for connectivity
- *School Computer Education Programme:* About 3600 secondary and senior secondary have been covered under this model on BOT basis and support is sought for extension of the programme after expiry of the BOT contract and for learning materials that will increase impact of computers deployed as also for connectivity.
- *Computer-Aided Learning Programme (CALP) :* Involving about 380 schools where the programme is presently

being implemented through assistance of the Azim Premji Foundation. Support is invited for expanding the programme beyond the current schools.

- *EDUSAT:* About 100 locations including Teacher Training Institutions are being made operational by the Indian Space Research Organisation. Support for creating content to utilize Edusat effectively and expanding number of locations with access is desirable.
- *Teacher Training Technology Academies:* Partnership with world-class ICT companies for effective skill upgradation for teachers is already in place and can be expanded to cover all the teachers in the State.
- *Departmental Computerisation:* All field level offices down to block level to be computerized. Support is required for data management and connectivity solutions and for making sure that the ICTs installed are used effectively.

Other potential ICT interventions could be:

- *Deploying and using ICTs in Primary Schools:* Especially to promote retention.
- *Mobile ICT Labs:* To promote retention in primary schools in remote areas, and minimize the digital divide that could arise between centrally located and remote schools.
- *Distance Learning for Teachers:* Increasing quality of teachers as a significant way of improving learning achievements.

Non-ICT Interventions to Enhance Enabling Environment and Provide Social Empowerment: The REI takes pride in asserting that apart from technology interventions, there shall be a clear focus on other aspects of schooling involving social responsibility commitments to help the underprivileged and deprived children gain access to the unlimited advantages of education sometimes taken for granted by other children placed in more advantageous positions in life. This human concern for the welfare of such children is perhaps the single most distinguishing feature of the REI.

Some of the Suggested Programmes Include:

- *Learning Skills Development:* Whereas access has been provided to a large extent and the question of teacher recruitment has been substantially addressed, the real issue is now of learning skills and competencies of the child. Effective competency development programmes with verifiable standards have to be put in place, especially in far flung areas of the State. This problem is, in fact, more acute in areas of the State inhabited by disadvantaged societies and also among some sections of the socially backward population. The MoU already in place with the Azim Premji Foundation is a good example to emulate as also the MoU with the Hole in the Wall Education Ltd., a subsidiary of NIIT.
- *Adoption of Schools:* Adoption of schools for both capital cost by way of construction and recurring cost for management has been proposed by the Education Department. A MoU model to cater to the individual adoption pattern of potential donors has already been put in place. There is much scope for the corporate sector to accept this programme
- *Scholarships for Indigent Children:* Many foundations and charitable organizations are coming forward to provide stipend for indigent, but bright, children to pursue their studies. The examples set by the Akshaya Patra Foundation and the Foundation for Excellence are noteworthy. Again, this is an area for wide-scale replication.
- *Mid-day Meals Programme:* Improving the quality of the mid-day meals offered to enhance nutrition and to attract more children to come to school for the meals. There is a viability gap between current levels of provisioning by the Government of India and the State Government towards this programme and the actual requirement of a quality meal with adequate calorific value. This gap is now being made good by some selected foundations such as

Akshaya Patra and is certainly adaptable in a big way in all the primary schools in the State.

- *Children with Special Needs:* Although there is a funding within the Sarva Shiksha Abhiyan for this purpose, there is much that is desired to be done. The numbers of voluntary organizations working in this sector are required to be enhanced with corporate assistance. The State Government has announced scholarships for all girl children with disabilities in classes IX to XII. There is unlimited potential to take this programme further. It is not out of place to mention here the MoUs signed with Bodh Shikshan Sansthan for deprived slum children. In the same vein, the MoU with the international foundation Educate Girls Globally (EGG) for enrolment and retention of girls in schools is also a noteworthy beginning.
- *Health and Sanitation:* Within the overall framework of the Total Sanitation Campaign, an ambitious programme has been taken up for providing over 40,000 schools with water and sanitation facilities within the next three years with the active involvement of the State Public Health Engineering Department and the UNICEF.

Cross-cutting Issues:

- Teacher Training - It is an undisputed fact that the only real way to improve quality of education in schools is to have well qualified and motivated teachers with periodic training for skill upgradation. Such training programmes should equip them to be competent to accept technological changes in teaching methodology and also improvement in pedagogical competencies. The teacher training programmes that will be initiated with the MoUs now in place with ICT leaders such as Microsoft, Intel and Cisco will serve as models for all training programme in the State. It has also been observed that there is adequate funding for such programme within the Sarva Shiksha Abhiyan and this can be skillfully clubbed with the expertise available with the ICT companies.

- *Curriculum:* Along with the increasing deployment of ICT in schools, the need for introduction of Computer-Aided Learning Programme has become apparent. There is an on-going debate on the kind and quality of e-curriculum that is required for adoption in schools. The curriculum has to be tailored to the specific needs of the educational system of the State while enabling children to understand concepts and important basic instructional inputs that will have a long-lasting impact on the mental growth of the student. There are adequate and large numbers of such software available in the market and a judicious decision will have to be taken while examining the issues related to curriculum.
- *Infrastructure:* It is realized that there are again funds available for creation of infrastructure for schools in the Sarva Shiksha Abhiyan, which is for education up to the level of elementary, although there is a constraint of funds in the secondary and senior secondary stage of education. The involvement of the corporate sector for such requirements can be examined under the REI along with the resources of the State Government.

GOVERNANCE AND MANAGEMENT

The governance and management of the Rajasthan Education Initiative must adhere to three central principles:

- Accord the leading role to the Government of Rajasthan, recognising its primacy in setting objectives for education on behalf of its people, the leadership and enterprise already displayed by its political leadership and bureaucracy, and the public finance that has already been dedicated to the REI.
- Ensure independence of the fundamental governance of REI from partners involved in individual projects that are catalysed by and operate under the REI.
- Be responsive to, and seek out, appropriate inputs from all partners involved in REI projects, so that REI governance and management is able to optimize the

environment for those projects and maximise their chances of success.

While specific details of governance and management remain to be finalised by the State Government and the other core partners, the Rajasthan Education Initiative will have governing bodies to supervise the REI and a Programme Management Office to oversee implementation.

The Programme Management Office will be responsible for the day-to-day administration of the REI with responsibility for recruiting partners, filtering proposals for projects, oversight of implementation of projects and for helping resolve issues, managing relationships with partners, evaluation of project impact at the end of project period, dissemination of findings and enabling scaling up where appropriate. The structure of the Office should be lean and small to ensure efficiency with appropriate delegation of powers and authority at different levels. It may consist of Programme Director, Programme Coordinator, and Programme Officers - appointed by the Government of Rajasthan. Experts may be hired, or tapped from outside partners, to advise on education, ICTs, PPP frameworks, and monitoring & evaluation. GeSCI's Facilitator will act as an advisor to the REI Programme Director and Programme Coordinator.

Each approved project should put in place appropriate management structures to ensure delivery, which will be the responsibility of the private sector or other partners involved. The Government of Rajasthan recognises that it will need to appoint project liaisons for each specific project launched under REI, in addition to it responsibility for assigning staff to the PMO. Furthermore, the Government will need to allocate the time and energies of people at district and school levels to work on, and ensure coordination between, projects at local levels and the private sector playing an effective role.

FUNDING

In addition to the budgetary resources of the Government of Rajasthan, funds from the Government of India, and financial contributions from private sector partners, other sources of funding for the REI and its projects could include donor funding, community funding through Panchayats, and institutional finance including loans, among others.

EVALUATION OF THE REI

The REI shall develop a suitable evaluation framework, which will reflect the stated vision and roles for the initiative and measure impact on key issues of Rajasthan's Education System. The evaluation will assist in adjusting implementation strategies as the initiative progresses.

PROGRAMME FOR ENRICHMENT OF SCHOOL LEVEL EDUCATION

The PESLE partners are making strategic interventions in the government-run-school system. This includes linking up with larger scale education reform programmes like the District Primary Education Programme (DPEP), the Joint Government of India-United Nations (GOI-UN) Programme and the Sarva Shiksha Abhiyan Programme, among others.

Bodh Shiksha Samiti works closely with the Government of Rajasthan on education reforms in elementary education including pre-school education. Bodh has also been asked by the Government of Jammu and Kashmir to play a major technical assistance role in re-structuring the management and content of its primary school system. While the Aga Khan Education Service, India (AKES, I) engages with schools of the Municipal Corporation of Mumbai, Dr. Reddy's Foundation (DRF) continues with its long-term collaboration with the Andhra Pradesh State Education Department and the State police force. Similarly in Rajasthan, the Society for All Round Development (SARD) works with the government's education institutions to initiate education for first generation learners from marginalised Meo-Muslim communities.

In Hyderabad and urban Ranga Reddy district (Andhra Pradesh), DRF's Child and Police Project is working in collaboration with the Government of India's Sarva Shiksha

Abhiyan (SSA), in select State government schools since June 2003 on improvement of classroom processes for the rehabilitation of street and working children through Bridge schools (non-formal alternative education centres). DRF has also been invited by the Government to work in five mandals (blocks) of Hyderabad district, to improve access, learning achievement and stake-holders' participation in the school development process. Based on the positive outcomes emerging from the five mandals, the State government has requested DRF to replicate its interventions in eight additional districts of Andhra Pradesh.

The Government realises that in order to make the education innovations sustainable, key resource persons such as trainers and master-trainers need to emerge from within the system itself so that the learnings may be transferred into the system directly. Therefore, the state government is enabling the professional development of key resource persons and senior teachers by deputing them to the DRF CAP project. To take this forward, the 'Bridge School Training of Trainers' module developed by DRF has been accepted by the Education department to be used in the bridge schools in the State.

In Bharatpur District in Rajasthan, SARD has been cooperating closely with the Government of India's District Primary Education Programme (DPEP) in order to mainstream its education model in 20 government and private primary schools. Regular teacher-training sessions for the DPEP are conducted by SARD and so far, over 350 teachers have been trained. SARD has also placed a teacher in a school in Gadabaas at the request of the government.

SARD has also conducted a balika shivir (adolescent girls' camps) in collaboration with the DPEP last year in a joint programme in three villages in the district to encourage out-of-school and dropout girls aged 6-14 years to enable them to enrol in school. DPEP personnel, government school teachers and Panchayati Raj Institution representatives also joined the SARD programme staff and teachers as camp resource persons and organisers.

As part of an effort to impact the wider education system and go beyond their respective home states, the PESLE partners also provide inputs on teaching learning material development and school development processes to various non-profit organisations across the country. Thus, the programme, through its 'outreach' partners, has been contributing to government and private education systems and institutions in states as diverse as Himachal Pradesh, Assam, Uttar Pradesh, Tamil Nadu, Andhra Pradesh, Maharashtra, Gujarat, Madhya Pradesh, Rajasthan and Jammu and Kashmir.

JANSHALA

Accessible Education: A Reality

Rajasthan, educationally the second most backward state in the country, saw the formal launching of the Janshala Programme on 19 September 1998, with the registration of the Rajasthan Sahari Kachchi Basti Janshala Samiti, under the Societies Registration Act. The Chairman of the Executive Committee of the Samiti is the Special Secretary, Education, Government of Rajasthan, while the State Project Coordinator is the Secretary.

The Janshala effort in Rajasthan complements other ongoing activities in the field of elementary education, such as the Shiksha Karmi Project, the Lok Jumbish Project, the Guru Mitra Yojna, DPEP and NFE.

It aims to make elementary education increasingly accessible and effective for deprived children between 6-14 years of age in urban slums across the state. To this end, 10 zones have been identified in four cities: six in Jaipur (Vidyadhar Nagar, Hawamahal West, Hawamahal East, Civil Lines, Moti Dungri and Sanganer), two in Ajmer, and one each in Kishangarh and Bharatpur. NGOs are expected to play a major role in meeting assessed needs of the targeted population in these zones. NGOs have also been involved with running Alternative Schools called Samudayik Janshalas (SJs) and conducting base line assessment studies in Ajmer, Kishangarh and Bharatpur.

Activities and Achievements (1998-1999)

The activities that have been carried out, thus far, are as follows:

- The State Programme Management Unit has been set up and the staff recruitment process has started.
- Six zonal programme officers have been identified and specific zones assigned to them.
- Zonal Offices are being set up in upper primary school premises.
- The process of setting up of Cluster Resource Centres has started in each zone, and 8-10 schools will be covered in each cluster.
- Formation of the Zonal Level Programme Implementation Committee has already been initiated, and identification of zone-wise resource personnel has begun as well.
- The State Project Office has completed a base line survey of the six zones, on the basis of which it has been decided to target the slum clusters in these zones. Two hundred and nineteen slum clusters have been identified, of which only 74 have government school facilities. Approximately, 56,720 children in these slums have no school facilities or do not go to school, assuming that one does exist in the vicinity. A two-pronged strategy is, therefore, needed to meet the needs and requirements of the slum children:
  i. To empower the existing schools in the slums, and
  ii. Under-utilised non-functional government schools, situated in non-slum areas, will be transferred to the slums.
- Samudayik Janshalas will be set up in areas where there are a large number of deprived children and which are lacking government schools. Phase I will see the setting up of about 32 such schools in the first year, 46 in the second year and 78 in the third year. The number of such schools, designated as Rajkiya Janshalas (RJs), would be around 91 in Phase I. Thus, Samudayik Janshalas are

community schools which tap the resources of the community towards education, while Rajkiya Janshalas were existing schools that were transformed into community schools.

Other than the above, two meetings of the Executive Committee have been held and a core group has been formed under the Chairmanship of the Secretary, Shiksha Karmi Board in Jaipur, for developing MIS. The Bodh Shiksha Samiti, an NGO working in urban slums for the last 11 years, has been identified as the State Technical Resource Group. The Samiti has submitted Annual Work Plan cost estimates for 1999-2000, while UNICEF has transfer funds amounting to Rs. 10.80 lakhs for preparatory activities.

A Technical Resource Committee has been set up to review the activities of the State Technical Resource Group and give advice on the technical activities under this programme. The Janshala Programme in Rajasthan focusses mainly on:

- Improving the performance of teachers belonging to both Samudayik and Rajkiya Janshalas; adequate and appropriate utilisation of modern, interactive, child-centred and gender-sensitive techniques of teaching in multigrade classroom situations; and eventually bringing about an attitudinal change among the teachers.
- Addressing age-old social issues which adversely affect student enrolment and retention rates, as well as the performance of school children in the age group of 6-14 years.
- Achieving universalisation of elementary education in selected zones through concerted additional interventions, convergences and by the integration of education, health and other allied services.
- Focusing on problems faced by children belonging to the marginalised sections of society, especially girls, between the 6-14 age group in selected zones. This will hopefully, improve the enrolment rate as well as the retention and performance of these children in school.

- Assessing the educational needs of out-of-school adolescents, especially girls, and to provide educational opportunities to them.
- Evolving a system of work, based on school mapping, micro planning and continuous, sustained interaction between local communities and teachers, and make arrangements for their training as well.
- Providing and improving the available academic and resource support at both school and cluster levels by organising training/workshops for zone programme officers, resource persons, cluster heads, headmasters and teachers.
- Starting early child care education, an important support activity for elementary education in Samudayik Janshalas.
- Providing ample scope for conducting research and for the implementation of innovations.
- Enhancing the community's sense of programme ownership.

CHALLENGES AHEAD

- The selection of NGOs that are genuinely interested in the Janshala effort and sustaining their interest in programme implementation.
- The state government needs to ensure timely and continued placement of programme functionaries.
- To mobilise communities for effective participation in school management. It is very difficult to bring all the sections of the community under one umbrella because of the prevailing differences in the socio-cultural and economic conditions in urban areas.
- To effectively coordinate between so many partners in the existing formal system of elementary education in the state.

Keeping in view these challenges, it becomes necessary to develop both practical and emotional ties, based on work culture, with the teachers, community and NGOs. With regard to this, proper caring and sharing of the roles and responsibilities by all the partners can be of immense help. Rajasthan has always taken a keen interest and shown initiative in launching different types of innovative programmes, despite being the second most backward state in terms of literacy and education. The Janshala Programme is a bid to eradicate mass illiteracy and provide educational opportunities to the girl child and deprived children in the urban slums in Rajasthan.

STUDY ON EDUCATING ADOLESCENT GIRLS

Brain Storming: The Joint GOI-UN System Education Programme emphasises the need to target girls, working children, children belonging to scheduled castes and scheduled tribes, minorities, disabled children, and children in selected remote areas to achieve UEE. In its endeavour to promote education for out-of-school adolescent girls and to map out educational opportunities that are available for this target group, it is proposed to conduct an experience study of educating adolescent girls in four states, namely: AP, Bihar, Rajasthan and UP. The proposed study would respond to a number of research questions, some of which are identified as follows:

- What were the constraints in education of adolescent girls?
- How were the adolescent girls and their parents motivated for education?
- What is the profile of the adolescents participating in the NFE programme?
- What is the profile of the organisation involved in the innovative scheme for educating adolescent girls?
- What efforts have been made by the organisation in creating a supportive environment for their education?
- What are the contents, materials and methodology of teaching them?
- What is the profile of teachers/para teachers and the contents, duration and methodology of their training?

- Whether linkages have been established with formal system/ continuing education?
- What are the academic achievements and level of general awareness as a result of participation in the programme?
- Are there arrangements for follow-up after participation in the NFE programme?
- What is the impact of participation in NFE on self, family and community?
- What are the perceptions/opinions of the adolescents, family and community about the NFE programme?
- Suggestions, if any, by adolescents, parents, teachers, and community for strengthening NFE programmes.

In order to discuss, finalise the scope and terms of reference of the proposed study and plan better for the education of out-of-school adolescent girls, a brainstorming session was held on 19th November 1998, in the National Programme Management Unit (NPMU) office at New Delhi. The participants were drawn from national and international NGOs of repute, which are currently engaged in promoting education through a gender-sensitive approach; the collaborating UN agencies, Government of Bihar and the GOI.

After a brief introduction by Mr. Suresh Kumar, National Programme Manager of the Joint GOI-UN System Education Programme, Dr. Sharada Jain, SRC Jaipur, opened the session. She said that the proposed study could explode some of the often-quoted prevalent myths about girls and community indifference for their education. She raised specific questions for consideration and response of the participants. Brainstorming method was used to facilitate rigorous questioning on the objectives, modes and expected outcomes of the study.

Question-based discussion in the session was as follows:

Do we need this study? How can it contribute to the Joint GOI-UN system Education Programme?

Most participants agreed that this kind of study is the need of the hour. Ability to plan depends upon the exposures available to planners. Broadening horizons is needed to facilitate appropriate decisions by block level programme managers to visualise alternatives.

Are there not enough existing studies, which could be used? What is the purpose of launching yet another study to add further to a sterile set of codification, which have not contributed to action interventions?

The group felt that though there are studies conducted by different organisations or programmes, they are limited and programme-specific. They are segregated, isolated, unanalysed experiences from which limited insights could be drawn in a programme such as the Joint UN Initiative, there is a need for user-friendly studies written in a manner by which it could be interpreted by the functionaries in their specific context. Analysis of the existing studies could be the starting point of this particular attempt.

Why study adolescent girls, when the project is dealing with primary education? How does this age group figure in the objective of this project?

Adolescence is an age, which needs specific attention, education and internment. And yet, it is this age group which is deprived of educational facilities. Whenever their education is brought into focus, it gets entangled with some routine perceptions of what the guardians feel. If their negative attitude was the ultimate fact, then one could never have got such a wide range of success stories across the country in the education of adolescent girls. People now know the kind of alternatives that are available to facilitate meaningful educational processes.

If understanding the operative factors for facilitating education for adolescents is so important, then why not include boys in this study?

Boys and girls need equal attention. It is also important to identify the roles that fathers, elders and brothers play in girls' education. However, given the fact that the educational scenario for girls is particularly grim, it may be desirable, as a first step, to begin with adolescent girls in focus and keep in mind the necessary supportive roles of men/boys in their educational journey. If the purpose of the study is to strengthen actual doer's, will the mode of codifying it include participation of project managers? It would be ideal, if it could be so, wherever possible. The study could also be conducted and documented in vernacular languages to capture full nuances of the processes. Translation in English should be a subsequent part of the whole exercise. Systematic efforts for dissemination and facilitating interpretation of the knowledge at the field level should be a planned step, in order to empower the local programme managers and implementers.

Why only success stories? Is it not equally important to codify failures? So many attempts have been made with no outcomes, would it not be equally important to codify them?

Failures should be recorded to inform what leads to what and should be avoided while implementing any plan to facilitate education. Success stories are analysed in a systematic way to ensure the understanding of what could, or would lead to total failure also. 'Success' itself clarifies that there was an absence of factors that could lead to failure. A positive approach can inspire in a fuller manner.

Should it be State-wise or Initiative-wise? The focus should be on significant initiatives, nationwide, as that would provide the necessary and sufficient backup for the planners to choose from. 'Successful initiatives' should be taken cognisance of, but considering the time dimension and the utmost need to feed these experiences to the functionaries at the block level, their respective states could be the first priority.

How can we get to know of significant initiatives across the country? For compilation of this basic information, it was decided that information on institution based initiatives would be compiled by UNICEF in collaboration with other UN agencies. Information regarding individual initiatives would be gathered by Ms. Vimala Ramachandran and Mr. Suresh Kumar with the assistance of all other members present in the meeting. This part would be completed within a fortnight.

Should it be confined to the rural areas or should it also include urban slum initiatives?

The study should not be limited to the rural areas only. In Andhra Pradesh and Rajasthan, the UN Programme is working in urban areas. And therefore, both rural and urban experiences should be looked at. The study should take cognisance of three levels of initiatives *viz.*, initiatives within the larger programmes; experiences generated through small NGO initiatives and individual struggles.

RAJASTHAN EDUCATION SYSTEM

The education scene of the state is changing frequently owing to the initiatives taken by the Government and the involvement of other institutions. For providing educational services, enrolment of students in schools, abbreviating gender disparities and promoting education, a number of policies have been implemented.

There has been a leap in the literary rate in the last ten years. The literary rate grew from 38 % in 1991 to over 61 per% in 2001. In the near future the state aims to attain a remarkable percentage of literacy rate, so the primary is free and mandatory and for all children in the state. At present the Education System of Rajasthan consists of nine universities and more than two hundred and fifty colleges, fifty five thousand primary and seven thousand four hundred secondary schools. The Rajasthan University Results normally come out in the months of November and December.

The state has forty-one engineering colleges with an annual enrolment of about 11,500 students. There are twenty-three polytechnics and one-hundred and fifty-two Industrial Training Institute (ITIs) that impart vocational training to the students. Rajasthan Technical Education Board in Jodhpur is engaged in imparting technical education and arranges for the Rajasthan Pre Entrance Test for Engineering, Architecture and Pharmacy known RPETEAP. The LNM Indian Institute of Information Technology at Jaipur was recently set up by the LN Mittal Foundation that belonged to the Ispat International group.

This institution provides technical education in the fields of IT, Electronics, Communication and other emerging technologies. The entire network of such educational institutes have resulted in the creation of a pool of educated, qualified and expert professionals to the Business industrial sectors in Rajasthan.

The medical institutes have also facilitated health to a great extent. In 1996-97 the Government of Rajasthan opened up Medical Education to the private sector. The state has eight medical colleges (two in the private sector while six in the public sector) with an annual intake of 700 students. There are eight Dental Colleges in the state with about an intake of 740 students. Apart from these there are twenty-eight pharmacy institutes where 1,600 students get enrolled annually. Rajasthan also has 26 Management Institutes with about 1,460 seats.

RAJASTHAN SCHOOLS

Education is highly valued in Rajasthan. The Government of Rajasthan is actively encouraging the people to send in their wards to school. Female education is highly stressed upon. Aap Ki Beti is a scheme which provides subsidized education, uniforms and other help to the female child of impoverished families. The Zila Prathamik Shiksha and Sarva Shiksha Schemes emphasize on the importance of primary education in the state. The number of government funded or aided schools in Rajasthan are as follows:

School/Office	*School Type*	*Rural/Urban*	*No. of Schools*
School	Senior Secondary	Rural	1413
School	Senior Secondary	Urban	577
School	Secondary	Rural	2988
School	Secondary	Urban	528
Office	Others	Rural	1
Office	Others	Urban	53
School	Others	Urban	1

Total Other Offices 54

Total Other School 1

Total Secondary Schools 3516

Total Senior Secondary Schools 1990

Apart from this other institutions and projects such as the Gramin Shiksha Kendra have aided in increasing the number of schools in rural areas.

Some of the leading schools in the state are:

School	*Location*	*Affiliation*	*Pupils*
Ajmer Military School	Ajmer	CBSE (XII)	Boys
Banasthali Vidyapith	Banasthali	SSC (XII)	Girls
Bharatiya Vidya Bhawan's Vidyashram	Jaipur	CBSE (XII)	Co-ed
Bhoruram Jiram Dass Public School	Churu	CBSE (XII)	Co-ed
Birla Balika Vidyapith	Pilani	CBSE (XII)	Girls
Birla Public School Vidya Niketan	Pilani	CBSE (XII)	Boys
Dholpur Military School	Dholpur	CBSE (XII)	Boys
Maharani Gayatri Devi Girls' High School	Jaipur	CBSE (XII)	Girls
Mayo College	Ajmer	CBSE (XII)	Boys
Mayo College Girls' School	Ajmer	CISCE (XII)	Girls
The Sagar School	Alwar	CBSE (XII)	Co-ed
Sainik School	Chittorgarh	CBSE (XII)	Boys

RAJASTHAN UNIVERSITIES

Higher education has been duly emphasized by the Government of Rajasthan and the workings of the department of education have been actively promoting the masses to educate their children beyond school level.

The University Grants Commission records show that about 3,63,172 young girls and boys have enrolled into colleges and universities in the year 2002-2003 and the number of women enrolling into such institutions has been exceptionally high too.

Bibliography

Banerjee, Indubhusan: *Evolution of the Khalsa*. Calcutta: A. Mukerjee, 1963.

Bhagat Lakshman: *Short Sketch of the Life and Works of Guru Gobind Singh*. Asian Educational Services.

Choudhary, J. N. : *Divorce in India Society*, Jaipur, Rupo Books, 1988.

Cole, William: *The Sikhs: Their Religious Beliefs and Practice*. Sussex Academic Press, 1995.

Cunningham, J.D.: *A History of the Sikhs*, Delhi, 1966.

Dikshit, D.P. *Political History of the Chalukyas of Badami*. New Delhi: Abhinav, 1980.

Fairservis, Walter A.: *The Roots of Ancient India: The Archaeology of Early Indian Civilization*, New York, Macmillan, 1971.

Gambhirananda, S.: *Brahma Sutra Shamkar Bhasya*, Adavita Ashrama, Calcutta, 1977.

Gerald, N. : *The Sikhs and Their Literature*, Delhi, 1970.

Habib, Irfan : : *An Atlas of the Mughal Empire*, New York: Oxford University Press, 1982.

Harbans Singh: *Berkeley Lectures on Sikhism*, Manohar Publication, Delhi, 1995.

Jain, Kailash Chand, *Lord Mahavira and His Times*, Saraswati Press, Delhi, 1974.

James, Lawrence: *The Rise and Fall of the British Empire*, St. Martin's, 1997.

Jasbir Kaur Ahuja: *The Zafarnama of Guru Gobind Singh*. Mumbai: Bharatiya Vidya Bhavan. 1996.

Jasbir Singh Ahluwalia: *The Doctrine and Dynamics of Sikhism*, Punjabi University, 2001.

John Clark: *The Sikhs*, Princeton, Delhi, 1946.

Kalika Prasad Tiwari: *Foundations of Ancient Indian Culture*, Pointer Publishers, Delhi, 2001.

Kapur, A, Rajiv: *Sikh Separatism : The Politics of Faith,* London, 1986.

Kartar Singh Bhalla: *Let's Know Sikhism : A Religion of Harmony, Brotherhood and Tolerance,* Star Publication, Delhi, 2002.

Koenraad Elst: *Who is a Hindu? : Hindu Revivalist Views of Animism, Buddhism, Sikhism and Other Offshoots of Hinduism,* Voice of India, 2002.

Lakshmanna, C.: *Caste Dynamics in Village India,* Nachiketa Publications, Bombay, 1973.

Lal, K.S. : *The Mughal Harem.* New Delhi: Aditya Prakashan, 1988.

Levy, Ruben: *The Social Structure of Islam,* Cambridge, 1957.

Mahajan, V. D.: *Muslim Rule In India.* S. Chand, New Delhi, 1970.

McLeod, W.H; *The Sikhs : History, Religion and Society,* New York, 1989.

Moreland, W.H.: *From Akbar to Aurangzeb,* London, 1923.

Moynihan, E. : *Moonlight Garden: New Discoveries at the Taj Mahal,* Delhi, 2001.

Nanda, Ratish, : *Delhi : The Built Heritage - A Listing* , Indian National Trust for Art and Cultural Heritage, 1999.

Nesbitt, Eleanor: *Sikhism: A Very Short Introduction,* Oxford University Press, USA, 2005.

Nikky Guninder and Kaur Singh: *Sikhism: An Introduction,* Viva Books, 2012.

Nirbani Singh: *Sikhism : Continuity of Indian Culture,* Kalpaz Publications, 2013.

Owen, Sidney J. : *The Fall of the Moghul Empire,* London, 1912,

Pelsaert, Francisco : *Jahangir's India,* Cambridge, 1925.

Prasad, Saksena Banarsi : *History of Shahjahan of Dihli,* Allahabad: The Indian Press, 1932.

Qaisar, Ahsan Jan : *Building Construction in Mughal India,* Delhi: Oxford University Press, 1989.

Qureshi, I. H.: *The Administration of the Mughals.* Lahore, 1944.

Rafiabadi, Naseem : *Islam and Sufism in Kashmir : Some Lesser Known Dimensions,* Sarup, Delhi, 2009.

Skelton, Robert : *The Indian Heritage: Court Life & Arts under Mughal Rule,* Delhi, 1982.

Index

K

L

M

P

R

S

T

V

W

❑❑❑